The Ancient Near East

E ORIGINS
OF
VILIZATION

The Ancient Near East

ANNIE CAUBET AND
PATRICK POUYSSEGUR

·TERRAIL·

Cover illustration
STATUE OF GUDEA SEATED
Second Dynasty of Lagash,
Telloh (formerly Girsu),
diorite,
height 46 cm (18 1/8 in).
Musée du Louvre, Paris.

Page 2
RELIEF FROM THE PALACE
OF KING ASHURBANIPAL
Detail. Assyrian empire, Nineveh,
Mosul marble,
82 x 51 cm (32 1/4 x 20 in).
British Museum, London.

This panel depicting a royal park
bears witness to Ashurbanipal's
desire to civilise his world – note the
complex irrigation system and the
colonnaded pavilion.

STATUE OF GUDEA WITHOUT
INSCRIPTION
Detail. Second Dynasty of
Lagash, Telloh (formerly Girsu),
diorite,
height 107 cm (42 1/8 in).
Musée du Louvre, Paris.

The hands are clasped in the traditional attitude signifying prayer.

Page 6
DISH WITH HUNTING SCENE
Detail. 14th-13th century BC,
Ugarit, gold,
diameter 18.8 cm (7 3/8 in).
Musée du Louvre, Paris.

The design shows the king in his
chariot hunting goats and bulls,
as proof of a mastery over nature
which had to be continually
reasserted.

Editorial director: Jean-Claude Dubost
Editor: Aude Simon
Editorial assistant: Geneviève Meunier and Claire Néollier
With the collaboration of: Ann Sautier-Greening and Béatrice Weité
English translation: Peter Snowdon
Cover design: Gérard Lo Monaco and Laurent Gudin
Graphic design: Véronique Rossi
Graphics for the table "From pictographs to cuneiform": Armelle Donval
Iconography: Patrick Pouyssegur
Typesetting and filmsetting: Einsatz Goar Engeländer, Paderborn
Photoengraving: Litho Service T. Zamboni, Verona.

© FINEST SA / ÉDITIONS PIERRE TERRAIL, PARIS 1997
The Art Books division of BAYARD PRESSE SA
English edition: © 1998
Publisher's number: 187
ISBN 2-87939-152-0
Printed in Italy

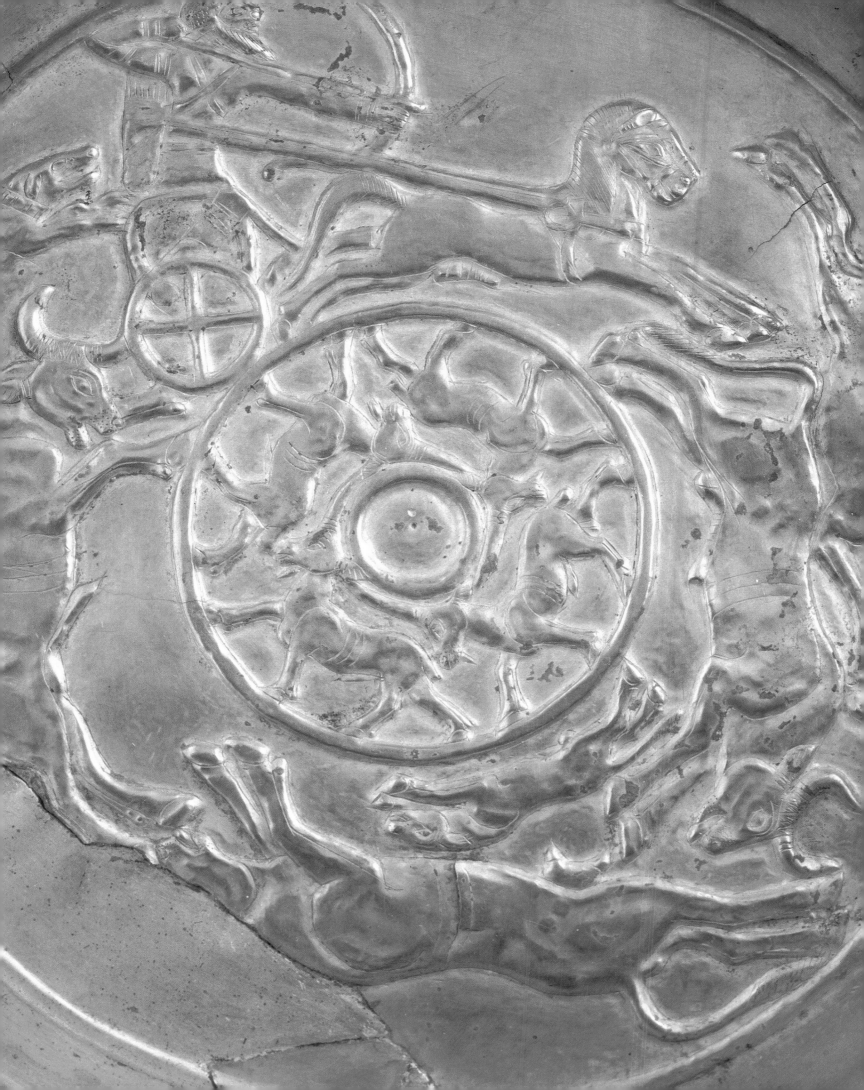

Contents

Introduction

JEBEL BISHRI
Countless Semitic peoples –
Akkadians, Amorites and
Aramaeans – passed through
this steppe, which dominates
the middle valley of the
Euphrates, on their way to the
rich flood plains of the twin
rivers of Mesopotamia.

The ancient Near East covered a vast area. Its heartlands alone occupied the Levant, Anatolia, Mesopotamia and Iran. Its influence spread with the Semitic peoples of the Mediterranean into North Africa. From Carthage, colonies reached out to embrace the islands to the north, Spain, and even the Atlantic coast. Neolithic cultures carried its mark deep into the Balkans and the Caucasus. The early trade routes that would later become the silk road acted as its vector throughout much of central Asia, as far as the borders of India and China. It was as long-lived as it was geographically extensive. Its history only begins with the invention of writing, in the 4th millennium BC, but this written history was preceded by a long period of cultural continuity that can be traced as far back as the 11th–10th millennia. Yet despite the vast scale on which they evolved, both in space and time, the cultures of the ancient Near East form an undeniable unity, thanks to certain underlying features which remain constant throughout every change.

The first of these features is spatial: a constant relationship uniting certain geographical regions – the Mediterranean coast; the great river valleys of the Tigris, the Euphrates, the Orontes and the Amu Darya; and the steppe (a more accurate term than "desert"), which was interspersed with fertile oases where human life had always flourished, thanks to the presence of certain wild animals (pigs, sheep, goats and cattle) and plants (corn, barley, lentils and others). It was the progressive domestication of these wild species which laid the foundations for the emergence of an agricultural society.

The second feature is temporal: a long-term process of evolution, in which innovations and inventions were gradually integrated into existing traditions, without ever entirely erasing the memory of the past. The geography and climate of the region conspired to encourage stable settlement, and urban centres such as Aleppo or Damascus were the capitals of their surrounding regions continuously for almost five thousand years. This gradualist approach to cultural change also applied to the domains of technology and the arts. The advanced metalworking techniques practised in ancient Mesopotamia – those used to make tableware and prestige weapons – could still be found in Damascus in the Middle Ages, to the point that the city's name was given to the technique of damascene work on metal. The crafts of fire – faience and glass – which appeared during the 3rd–2nd millennia would later become one of the great glories of Islam.

Coloured glazes were first used in buildings at Babylon and in Elam around the middle of the 2nd millennium. They were magnificently employed in the friezes of archers in Darius' palace at Susa in the 6th century BC. The technique was destined to flower again much later, producing an art of comparable beauty, in the ceramic decoration of countless mosques and palaces, from Isfahan to Samarkand.

Since ancient times, Europe has been in constant contact with the Near East. The relationship has often been a violent one, as it was during the period of the Crusades. But the Renaissance and the Enlightenment seem to have marked a turning point: henceforth, the world was to be possessed not by military conquest, but by knowledge. Diplomatic relations were established with the Ottoman Empire and Persia as early as the 16th century. The French consulate in Aleppo dates from the reign of François I. Travellers and scholars were motivated by a more or less vague conviction that the West owed a considerable debt to the civilisations of the East. For them, Eastern exoticism was not a mere mirage, or a dangerous threat, but a mask hiding the deeper truth of a relationship that had been evolving over many millennia. This curiosity was further stimulated by the arrival in Europe of the first inscriptions – an Aramaean stele that was transported to Carpentras, or a group of inscriptions from Palmyra. A votive cippus brought back from Malta enabled Abbé Barthélemy to break the code of the Phoenician language in 1758. This achievement marked the start of a long European tradition of studying oriental languages, grounded in a sound knowledge of biblical Hebrew.

However, those inscriptions that were brought back from Mesopotamia took much longer to render up the secret of the mysterious triangles and nails which gave their name to cuneiform writing ("cuneiform" means "wedge-shaped"). The "Michaux pebble" – in fact, a foundation document from Kassite Babylonia, now in the Bibliothèque nationale in Paris – was brought to France in 1786, but all the many early attempts to decipher it failed. Travellers returned with copies of cuneiform inscriptions they had found carved into the rocks above Lake Van in Turkey, on a cliff at Bisitun or in the ruins of Persepolis. The first copy of cuneiform signs to reach Europe had been brought back from Persepolis by the Italian Pietro Della Valle in 1621. In 1765, an intrepid German traveller, Carsten Niebuhr, returned with the first reasonably faithful copies of the Persepolis inscriptions and published them in an account of his journey, which was widely read at the time. These few clues were enough to fuel erudite speculation about vanished civilisations, and to raise doubts about the truth of what was then known of the history of the region, from the Bible and from Greek and Latin sources. The Middle Ages had spent much of its energy on trying to wrest Jerusalem, the scene of the Passion of Christ, from the Muslims. But what had become of the sites of the Old Testament – the tower of Babel, the ramparts of Nineveh or the city of Esther? The trail that was to lead to them began with these few incomprehensible signs. The "Rosetta stone" of cuneiform is the great text which Darius I had engraved on the cliffs at Bisitun in the province of Fars. On each side of the scene representing the king accepting the submission of his enemies are

Pages 10–11
THE CENTRAL ANATOLIAN PLATEAU
Part of the region known as the "Fertile Crescent", where wild species of barley and wheat sprang up in abundance at the end of the last ice age. The domestication of these plants was the determining factor in the passage from a subsistence economy to a productive economy.

THE BLACK OBELISK OF SHALMANESER III
Detail.

THE BLACK OBELISK OF SHALMANESER III
Detail. Assyrian empire, Nimrud (formerly Kalhu),
basalt,
height 198 cm (78 in).
British Museum, London.

The stone is decorated on all four sides with small reliefs depicting peoples who had been defeated in battle by the Assyrians paying tribute.

PERSIAN ARCHERS

Achaemenid Dynasty, Susa,
glazed brick,
475 x 375 cm (187 x 147 5/8 in).
Musée du Louvre, Paris.

Four archers of the royal guard are
shown standing on either side of a
cuneiform inscription in Babylonian,
Elamite and Old Persian, the official
languages of the empire.

| Pages 14–15
PERSIAN ARCHERS
| Detail.

carved many columns of parallel text. Each is clearly in a different language and script, but all use cuneiform. It was an Englishman, Henry Creswicke Rawlinson, who had been posted to the region as part of a military mission, who made the first faithful copy of these inscriptions, hanging from a rope let down from the cliff top in order to reach them. The results of his exploit were published in 1846. This paper provided the impetus which the study of cuneiform had been waiting for. Scholars in Germany and in Ireland, in London and in Paris pored over Rawlinson's copies; academic journals were flooded with articles offering divergent interpretations. One of the texts was identified as being a predecessor of modern Persian, designated as Old Persian. In this text, a certain group of signs was repeated over and over again. The hypothesis was advanced that this was the name of a king, most probably Darius. The hypothesis proved to be correct, and soon the first of the languages of Bisitun had been deciphered.

Progress with understanding Chaldean (or, as it is now known, Akkadian), the second language Darius had employed, was aided by a series of discoveries made at Khorsabad by Paul-Émile Botta from 1842 on. Botta was a young man who had been appointed French consul at Mosul. With the help of the artist Eugène Flandin he excavated part of the palace which Sargon II had built at the centre of his capital. At first, Botta thought that he had discovered the site of Nineveh, and his first results were published under this title. The drawings which he circulated reproduced not only all the sculptures which he had discovered, but also the great quantity of cuneiform texts he had found in the palace. As a result, the number of known texts that were accessible to scholars in Europe multiplied overnight. Thanks to this wealth of material, the Akkadian language was soon deciphered in its turn. Then, in 1846, A. H. Layard discovered the black obelisk of Shalmaneser III at Nimrud. Beneath the figure of a leader prostrating himself at the Assyrian king's feet could be read the name of Jehu, king of Israel. From this point on, the relationship between the history of Mesopotamian civilisation and that of the Bible was firmly established.

The study of these civilisations and of their literatures is sometimes termed Assyriology, because the first texts to be deciphered were written in Assyrian. Ironically, it was through these same texts that the existence of the Sumerians was first rediscovered; only later were the sites of their cities located and their material remains excavated. The kings of Assyria used to call themselves, among other titles, "king of Sumer and Akkad". Thus the inventors of writing re-emerged into recorded history through the bragging of their rivals. It was Ernest de Sarzec, French consul at Basra, who first uncovered material evidence of their existence. Hearing of certain statues that had been found by Bedouin tribes in the southern deserts of Mesopotamia, he began the excavations at Telloh which were to resurrect the monuments of Gudea, prince of Lagash around 2120 BC, and with them the culture of Sumer. Thus it was gradually demonstrated that both the Bible and the literature of the classical world rested on a foundation that predated them by many thousands of years. Europe could now trace its cultural origins to peoples who had inhabited the Near East as long ago as the 4th millennium BC.

1. Origins

Human beings have lived in the Near East for at least the past one and a half million years, to judge by the oldest signs of their existence which have survived, at Tell Ubaidiya, to the south of Lake Tiberias. *Homo erectus* was the first of our ancestors to venture outside Africa, crossing the Sinai to colonise Asia and Europe. He was followed by *Homo sapiens neanderthalensis* who disappeared around 350,000 BC, to be in turn replaced by *Homo sapiens sapiens*. Throughout the Palaeolithic period, which lasted several hundred thousand years, man lived by hunting, fishing and gathering. He would follow the herds of wild animals on which he depended as they migrated, constructing temporary camps of tents or simple huts wherever he paused long enough.

This semi-nomadic way of life experienced a slow yet certain evolution. Man gradually learned to master his environment. The stone tools he manufactured became ever lighter and more effective. Significantly, the microlithic technology was developed much earlier in the Near East than anywhere else. Likewise, he began to establish a fixed geography of burial grounds and sacred places, whose symbolic value for the community helped create the sense of a defined and enduring territory.

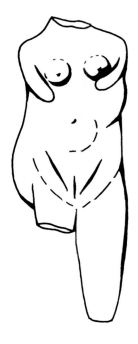

The first villages

The gradual evolution of Palaeolithic hunter-gatherer society made its first great leap forward in the wake of the change of climate that marked the end of the last ice age, around 15,000 BC. The climate of the Near East was henceforth both warmer and more humid. Wild cereals began to spring up in profusion at the foot of the great mountain chain that stretches from the hills of the Levant to the Taurus and the Zagros Mountains. This is the swathe of land which we know today as the "Fertile Crescent".

Men took advantage of these new conditions to settle permanently in one place. They gradually abandoned the caves and other shelters which nature had provided, and began instead to construct open-air terraces and small circular structures, modelled on the huts they had known before, but with their bases beneath ground level. The oldest of these settlements known today is at En Gev, near Lake Tiberias. Here stone mortars were used to grind grains, showing that wild cereals were being used as food.

From 12,500 BC onwards, small sedentary communities began to be established, which were obviously intended to be permanent. These are the first villages in history. Each of them is made up of a limited number of houses of modest dimensions, circular in form, partly sunk below ground level. At Mallaha in the Jordan valley, nine such houses have been found, their diameter varying between 3.5 and 5 metres (11 1/2 and 16 1/2 feet). A small stone wall shored up the side of the pit and was continued above ground level in lighter materials, probably branches, held in place by a circle of wooden poles. There must have been a few dozen houses in the village of Mallaha, which would have been home to a population of some two to three hundred people.

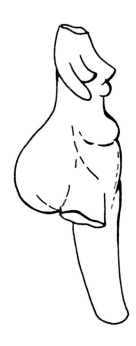

FEMALE FIGURINE
Early Neolithic baked clay figurines are amongst the first known examples of a tradition of representations of a female fertility principle. This tradition was long to play an important role, not only in the Near East, but throughout the Mediterranean region.

The houses were independent structures. Each generally had its own burial area, either directly under the floor or a short distance away. At Mallaha and at Hayonim, dogs have been found buried with their masters. This may have been a sacrificial practice, and is almost certainly a sign that these animals had been domesticated.

This trend towards sedentarisation continued throughout the Natufian period, from 12,500 to 10,000 BC. It had soon spread to the valley of the Orontes (Gerade) and the middle Euphrates (Abu Hureyra and Mureybet), and before long villages were to be found throughout the whole of the Fertile Crescent, from the Negev Desert to the Zagros Mountains.

One of the main factors which can be said for certain to have led to sedentarisation was the development of food storage techniques, in particular for wild cereals, which are easy to keep. The existence of silos for stocking grain and of grinding equipment bears witness to the increasingly central role played by this foodstuff in the Natufian economy. Yet the Natufian way of life remained highly diversified, and was everywhere adapted to suit local conditions. The Natufians were still essentially hunter-gatherers, as their art shows, with its predilection for animal figurines and for carved handles (in bone or stone) usually representing small herbivores, treated in a more or less realistic manner. Although some groups clearly established a fixed place of residence, others persisted in their traditional way of life, migrating with their prey.

Pages 18–19
SAMARRA PLATE
Detail. Late 7th–
early 6th millennium BC,
painted pottery,
Samarra culture,
diameter 27.7 cm (10 7/8 in).
Vorderasiatisches Museum, Berlin.

WILD OX HORN
10th millennium BC.
Mureybet, Syria.

This horn was found buried in a clay bench in one of the houses at Mureybet.

MODEL OF A PARTLY-SUNKEN
CIRCULAR HOUSE

10th millennium BC,
Mureybet, Syria.

Institute of Near Eastern Prehistory, Jales.

Yet despite the resistance of tradition, the invention of a sedentary way of life was to prove an irreversible step, which would lead to many radical changes in the structure of society. As such, it was merely the first stage in a profound transformation affecting all aspects of human life – what archaeologists refer to as "Neolithicisation".

Building techniques were constantly progressing during this period. After 10,000 BC (the date which marks the beginning of the Khiamian period), houses were still built on a circular plan, but they now rested directly on the surface of the ground. They were no longer sunk in a pit; instead, their had proper walls of stone held together by mortar or pisé (compressed clay). This development is illustrated by the site of Nahal Oren, near to the Mediterranean coast, where seventeen round houses with stone walls have been excavated. Each has a fireplace at the centre of its single room. The houses are packed tightly together, on four ascending terraces.

The repertoire of tools also expanded with the invention of the arrowhead. The El Khiam type (named after the site which also gave its name to this period) is characterised by its small dimensions and by the notches made along its edges. Gradually, the arrowhead would replace the microlith as the main hunting tool, thus providing further proof that hunting remained the principal resource of the Khiamian population.

This material evolution was accompanied by parallel developments in the symbolic and conceptual domains. At Mureybet on the middle Euphrates, the Natufian village (level I-A) was replaced by a Khiamian village (levels I-B and II). Bucranes and ox horns have been found buried in some of the clay benches that furnished these houses, while portable art consisted predominantly of female figurines carved somewhat schematically out of pebbles. These two symbols – the woman and the bull – are the well-springs of much of later Near Eastern theology, and already at this period they seem to have been endowed with some special merit, though they are not in any way personified and so cannot be considered as gods. Rather, they seem to have been cherished as the general symbolic principles under-lying a new way of life. As such, they must have helped the Khiamian people to articulate some of their central concerns. As humans began to lead sedentary lives that revolved around a fixed place of habitation, so they began to look for ways of ensuring the stability of their environment and the survival of their group.

The birth of agriculture

These developments in the domain of the imagination were to prove prophetic of a decisive change in the human way of life. This change defines the following period of prehistory, generally referred to by the abbreviation PPNA (Pre-Pottery Neolithic A). It lasted for almost a millennium, from approximately 9500 BC to 8700 BC. It was during this period that the first experiments were conducted in domesticating and cultivating wild cereals, principally wheat and barley. The Fertile Crescent was well endowed with species which lent themselves to domestication, and sedentarisation provided the conditions under which people could begin to observe the natural cycle, as both continuity and change. From such observations, it was but a short step to learning how to select and breed those varieties of plants which were best suited to cultivation. The result was the first act of human selection, which led to the cultivation of einkorn wheat and starch wheat. The latter is particularly well represented in the PPNA levels of the site at Aswad in the Damascus oasis – a region in which we can be certain that the plant did not originate. Domestication was not confined to grains, either: peas, chick peas, lentils, beans and vetch are also known to have been cultivated during this period.

Modern agriculture, founded on the double ritual of sowing and harvest-ing, thus has its origins in that privileged part of the Levant that stretches from the Jordan to the middle Euphrates. There, the first fixed settlements developed into agrarian communities, which could support an expanding population thanks to the control they now exercised over their food supply. The opportunistic economy of hunting slowly but surely gave way to a productive economy. Humanity was beginning to take control of its natural environment.

This development is confirmed by the disappearance of microlithic tools from the sites of this period, and the appearance in their place of countless scythe blades. Likewise, the high level of pollen deposits that have been found at sites such as Mureybet are a sure sign that there were cultivated fields close by. At this period, the population of villages was rising fast, due both to the development of agriculture itself, and to the influx of nomadic populations attracted by this new way of life. As a result, some of the villages grew into what were in effect small towns. One example is Jericho in the valley of the Jordan, which was already at this time surrounded by an impressive stone wall and dominated by a tower over 8 metres (26 feet) high with an inside staircase to reach the top. Such constructions could only have been realised through the collective mobilisation of an entire community, which in turn implies the existence of a recognised authority that could have organised the execution of such a project.

In both towns and villages, houses were becoming larger. Though their overall shape was still circular, they began to incorporate straight-edged forms in the division of their interior space, as at Mureybet III-A, which dates from the second half of the 10th millennium. The village is made up of round pisé houses, either built at ground level or partly sunk into the ground, spread over an area of no more than two or three hectares (roughly five to seven acres). The interior walls of these houses met at right angles, creating a series of functional spaces each of which was intended for a particular domestic activity: an entrance hall, a main room with a large clay bench, a "kitchen" with a hearth, and storage areas. It is only in Mureybet III-B, which dates from the early 9th millennium, that the first rectangular structures make their appearance. Built out of soft stone, they are made up of a number of square cells, all of which are too small for human habitation. Doubtless, these buildings were meant to serve as store houses.

It is also at Mureybet that we find the first evidence of experiments in baking clay. The objects produced were ritual objects – small vases or figurines. Female figurines were again very popular, whether schematic representations concentrating on the woman's sexual characteristics or more elaborately worked objects emphasising the fullness of the figure's forms. There is also evidence of another ritual practice emerging during PPNA: the so-called "skull cult", which was based on the removal of the skull from certain corpses after they had been buried. These skulls were then exhibited indoors, before being buried once again in a collective ritual. This practice has been well-documented at Jericho. It is one of the first stages in the development of ancestor worship. As such, it serves to reinforce the family group's sense of territoriality, by reaffirming both its identity and its continuity through time.

In these early days, the agrarian economy did not spread beyond the "core zone" of the Levant. Even in this area, there was no common culture, but rather a multitude of local variations on the new theme. To the east, the Zagros Mountains were still largely inhabited by free-roaming hunters, who occupied small settlements only at certain seasons. In northern Mesopotamia, on the other hand, round-house villages similar to those of the Levant were beginning to spring up (as at M'lefaat, Qermez Dere and Nemrik), but the economy that supported them remained clearly pre-agricultural.

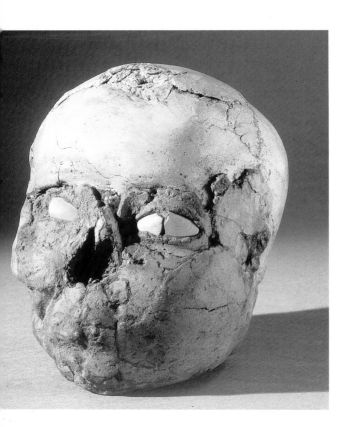

HUMAN SKULL
8th millennium BC, Jericho,
16 x 13 cm (6 1/4 x 5 1/8 in).
British Museum, London.

The face has been reconstructed in plaster, and the eyes replaced by shells. The hair and beard are painted. Such skulls probably served for some form of ancestor worship.

HUMAN SKULL
8th millennium BC, Jericho.
Amman Museum, Jordan.

The rise of agricultural society

PPNA was followed by PPNB (Pre-Pottery Neolithic B) around 8700 BC. The new productive economy was constantly progressing, colonising new geographical areas. This period of Neolithic expansion lasted for over one millennium and a half, until around 7000 BC. It has been divided into several phases: Early PPNB, Middle PPNB and Late PPNB, sometimes subdivided to define a Final PPNB. During the Early PPNB phase – which is so far the least well-understood – the way of life that had developed during PPNA spread from the middle Euphrates area towards the foothills of the Taurus Mountains. In doing so, it was travelling, in the opposite direction, the path taken by the obsidian that was imported from the Anatolian mountains. Populations migrated through the upper valleys of the Tigris and Euphrates, settling in the most favourable spots for cultivation (such as Dja'de, Nevali Çori, Çayönü Tepesi and Çafer Hüyük). The result was a distinctive Taurus culture, deriving from the culture of the middle Euphrates. The best example of this way of life is at Mureybet IV-A.

The most characteristic feature of PPNB culture is the increase in the number of rectangular buildings, now used for houses as well as for storage space. During the Middle PPNB (8200–7500 BC), the rectangular, multi-room house became the norm. The use of dried and shaped bricks for building encouraged this trend, which in turn lent itself to the diversified and hierarchical organisation of space. It also made it easy to extend existing buildings at will, by simply adding on further rooms.

The social changes which had brought about this new distribution of domestic space also changed the way communal space was organised. At certain sites, such as Çayönü Tepesi and Nevali Çori, buildings for the use

STATUE FROM AIN GHAZAL
8th millennium BC,
Jordan,
gypseous plaster,
height 105 cm (41 3/8 in).
Musée du Louvre, Paris.

STATUE FROM AIN GHAZAL
Detail.

VIEW OF ÇAYÖNÜ TEPESI
The architecture of this village, situated beside a tributary of the Tigris in eastern Turkey, is typical of PPNB building.

Pages 28–29
STAG HUNT

Detail. 7th millennium BC,
wall painting from a house
at Çatal Hüyük.

Ankara Museum, Turkey.

FEMALE STATUETTE

7th millennium BC,
Çatal Hüyük, Turkey,
baked clay.

Ankara Museum, Turkey.

The attitude of this obese woman
suggests she is about to give
birth, as befits a fertility goddess.
Her hands rest on the heads of
two panthers.

of the whole community were constructed on a square plan. These buildings were used for collective rituals, and were laid out with great care. They also housed the bodies of the dead, thus serving as a space where the living could enter into direct contact with their ancestors, sealing the continuity of the group over many generations. This practice was the collective equivalent of the family's "skull cult", which seemed to have been growing in importance. The skulls exhibited in the family home were now often painted, as at Mureybet IV-B, or even worked over again in another material, as at Jericho or Ramad, where faces were recomposed in plaster and eyes recreated out of inlaid shells, so as to give the impression of "life". At Ramad, the resulting objects were then placed on anthropomorphic pedestals. The statues modelled in plaster over a framework of reeds that have been found at Ain Ghazal and at Jericho would seem to have been associated with similar rites. As such, they would have been displayed in public, even though they were subsequently excavated from pits where they appear to have been buried.

The domestication of animals for use as a source of food represented a further significant step towards mastery over nature. The first animals to suffer this fate were the smaller ruminants: goats, and later sheep. They are docile creatures, which naturally stay together in herds, thus lending themselves to human control over their reproduction. In time, new species began to appear, which were smaller and more dependent upon man. Thus the domestic goat is descended from the pasang, and the domestic sheep from the oriental mouflon. These species were part of the agricultural repertoire by the beginning of the 7th millennium in various parts of the Levant, between the Jordan and the middle Euphrates, and possibly in the Zagros Mountains as well. During the early days of livestock farming, hunting was still practised – gazelles and big game were the usual prey – but it had already been superseded as the main source of animal protein. During the Middle PPNB, the agrarian way of life did not extend beyond the Levant and eastern Anatolia. It was still unknown to the sedentary communities of northern Mesopotamia, such as Nemrik. During the Late and Final PPNB (7500–7000 BC and 7000–circa 6500 BC), however, it continued to spread. It colonised the Mediterranean coastline, including the sites of Ras Shamra and Byblos, and began to make headway into the more hostile environment of the Syrian desert, at Buqras, close to the Euphrates, and at the oasis of El Kowm. This expansion was made possible by man's newly-acquired mastery of the natural environment. It was made necessary by the growth of the populations inhabiting the northern Levant, which led to constant pressure to increase the size of existing settlements and to develop new ones. In the northern Levant itself, villages proliferated, ever larger and more elaborate in their organisation. The first structured tracks appear, though they are not yet streets in any proper sense of the term. Rectangular houses are the norm, and their interior plan is generally quite simple. One original architectural form did emerge, however, first at Buqras, and later at El Kowm. This was a rectangle which was divided into three sections along the long axis. To either side are two groups of smaller rooms which are used as service areas. Between them is a large central hall, sometimes T-shaped, which is equipped with a hearth and several recessed alcoves. The entrance to the house is through a small room in one corner of the building, where a staircase or ladder leads to the terraces above. These form a large open-air area, which has a light well in the centre to illuminate the central hall.

This innovative design also involved the use of plaster or lime to cover the floors and the walls. These materials, which are obtained by heating gypsum or limestone, imply an advanced, high-temperature technology. They were also used to make all sorts of vessels, known as "white ware", but which soon proved to be too fragile for daily use. It was replaced by a new technique that emerged during the Recent PPNB period: ceramic production. This method was invented more or less simultaneously in Syria, Anatolia and the Zagros region. Using baked clay, objects could be created that were much more varied in form, as well as much more robust. The earliest ceramics use a shiny light-coloured paste, and some pieces even have painted decorations. Metalworking was also increasingly a focus of interest, especially in mineral-rich areas. At that time, metal was worked cold with a hammer: for example, copper at Çayönü Tepesi, which was close to the rich copper mines of eastern Anatolia. The small objects produced in this way – beads and pins –, usually in copper or lead, are quite rare. However, they soon came to play an important role in trade, and can be found at sites that are far from any natural source of minerals – at Ramad, for example.

Networks of communication between the different human communities of the Near East flourished during the Recent PPNB, and the agrarian way of life spread ever further from its heartlands. New, more difficult, species of stock were domesticated, including types of cattle and pig. Agricultural communities emerged in northern Mesopotamia, under the influence of the PPNB cultures of the Taurus region and Syria. One such community was the village of Maghzaliyah, at the foot of the Jebel Sinjar. There the inhabitants made "white ware", and covered the walls and floors of their rectangular houses with a gypsum-based coating. During a later phase, an impressive defensive wall was erected out of huge blocks of limestone, an exceptional structure for an agricultural settlement. The new way of life continued to spread to the east, as far as the valleys of the Zagros region, where pre-pottery agricultural communities were also founded (at Qal'at Jarmo or Tepe Guran, for example). To the south, it now extended as far as the plains at the foot of the Susiana and Deh Luran hills.

The beginning of the 7th millennium, however, saw what appears to be a retreat from the new culture and technologies in the southern Levant. Large buildings were abandoned in favour of small structures, which were doubtless only inhabited on a seasonal basis. A pastoral nomadic way of life emerged in the desert steppes of the interior, based on migratory herding of sheep and goats. Yet the culture of the northern Levant was still in an expansionist mood. New settlements were established on the Mediterranean coast, from Byblos as far afield as Mersin in Cilicia. The island of Cyprus, which is only a hundred kilometres (about 60 miles) from the Levantine coast, was colonised by continental populations who brought

JAR
Detail.

JAR
7th millennium BC,
Tell Hassuna,
baked clay.
Iraq Museum, Baghdad.

The geometrical design cut into the surface is typical of the Hassuna culture.

PLATE

6th millennium BC,
Tell Arpachiyah,
polychrome pottery,
Halaf culture,
diameter 33 cm (13 in).
Iraq Museum, Baghdad.

PLATE

Late 7th–early 6th millennium BC,
Iraq,
painted pottery,
Samarra culture,
diameter 27.7 cm (10 7/8 in).
Vorderasiatisches Museum, Berlin.

**The design depicts birds fishing,
with a swastika-type symbol at
the centre.**

their domesticated plants and animals with them. Thus the agrarian way of life, that would eventually permeate the entire continent of Europe, began to spread north and west through the islands of the Aegean Sea and the Balkans.

Anatolia probably played an essential role in this process of dissemination. The site of Çatal Hüyük, located at the centre of the high plateau which covers the best part of the peninsula, was the scene of considerable activity around 7000 BC. It was then that the village grew into a substantial small town covering an area of some 12 hectares (almost 30 acres). It grew wealthy by trading in obsidian from mines in the surrounding volcanic mountain chains. A fairly large population lived there in houses made of unbaked brick, densely packed together. There were no roads; people got about by walking across the terraced roofs. Some of these houses were richly decorated with wall paintings and moulded clay reliefs. There were, once again, two dominant motifs in this art – the bull, which figured forcefully in the paintings, and whose horns and bucranes were hung on walls and pillars, and a powerful woman depicted with much-exaggerated forms, sculpted in high relief on the walls or as a statuette in the round. She was usually shown in the act of giving birth, but might also be represented as the mistress of wild animals. These were, of course, the great symbolic themes that had first emerged in the Levant 3000 years previously – the bull and a woman who was ever more obviously a fertility goddess, mistress of life and death. Their importance in the Near East, and throughout the Mediterranean world, would continue to grow for many thousands of years yet to come.

The first ceramic cultures

The technique of ceramic production had appeared in the Near East at the end of the 8th millennium, and was widely practised by the beginning of the 6th millennium. It was a simple material innovation, which had no overwhelming effect on the lives of the agricultural communities of the region. It is important to modern archaeologists primarily because of the diversity of forms and decorative styles to which it gave rise. Thanks to the consistency with which each style was practised by the group with which it is associated, pottery has become the principal means by which we can distinguish between different cultures, prior to the invention of writing. Yet we should always bear in mind that these distinctions are only ever cultural distinctions. It is impossible to determine ethnic identities for periods that are so far in the past.

By studying the evolution of ceramic art in northern Mesopotamia, we can identify three successive cultures in the course of the 7th millennium: Umm Dabaghiyah, Hassuna and Samarra. The Umm Dabaghiyah culture lasted through the first half of the millennium. It was a direct descendent of the pre-pottery agrarian culture of Maghzaliyah, which in turn was derived from the Syrian PPNB. There are many features at Umm Dabaghiyah which still recall the Syrian PPNB: the square plan of the houses, for example, or the use of plaster as a building material. The houses are small, and some have wall paintings in which cattle can be seen, along with human figures. They are arranged in a ring around a number of large rectangular buildings, which were used to store the harvest. The pottery of this culture was simply made, and decorated with basic painted geometric motifs or reliefs representing cattle and snakes.

The Hassuna period covers the second half of the millennium. Its pottery is hardly more elaborate than that of Umm Dabaghiyah, and its decoration is still mainly dependent upon geometric motifs, either carved into the material or applied in brown paint. Both the pottery and the surviving houses show clearly that the Hassuna culture was a direct extension of the Umm Dabaghiyah culture. During this time, many small villages sprang up, as the methods of mixed cereal and livestock farming spread towards the Zagros Mountains and south along the valley of the Tigris.

The Samarra culture began in the middle of the Hassuna period, around 6200 BC. This new culture also spread to the south, reaching eventually as far as the vast Mesopotamian flood plain, at the very climatic limit of dry-land farming. The Samarra culture is distinguished by the high quality of

its ceramics, with their complex forms, light-coloured paste and meticulously smooth surfaces. Executed in black paint, the decorative designs bear witness to a genuine aesthetic and symbolic system. Their dynamic compositions use a number of stylised forms: circles of women dancing with their hair streaming out behind them, or whirling animals – goats, birds and fish – as well as purely geometrical figures. But the single greatest progress made at this time was in architecture: for the first time, moulded brick became widely used as a building medium. This represented a major change in living conditions for these small agricultural communities who already knew how to raise a number of different animals (cows, sheep, goats, pigs and dogs), and may even have practised some rudimentary form of irrigation. Although their villages were still small-scale communities, they were increasingly built according to standardised methods and forms.

The site of Tell es-Sawwan on the east bank of the Tigris is typical of this new kind of planned settlement. It is made up of a small number of large houses built out of moulded unbaked brick. Each house is divided into three parts, according to a plan that can be found as far back as Syrian PPNB. Each of these spacious structures was probably intended to house a single extended family. The houses are separated by large empty spaces, in which there is sometimes a small granary. During a second phase of building, the need for greater security led the villagers to construct a substantial perimeter wall and a ditch. The surface area of the houses, which were now gathered within this compound, was halved, but they were still built on a uniform plan, in this case T-shaped. In a final phase, the houses spread beyond the now demolished wall, bearing witness to the community's subsequent expansion.

Such uniform architecture implies that the village was an essentially egalitarian society. This is confirmed by the uniformity of its burial rites, as revealed by the tombs in the older levels of Tell es-Sawwan. They were dug directly beneath the houses, and contained a rich hoard of funerary objects, including many small statuettes, of which the great majority represent women. Carved out of alabaster, a precious material brought from the nearby Zagros Mountains, they have been carefully polished. The eyes are picked out in bitumen and often inlaid with shell. Represented naked, these women – in keeping with the long tradition which originated in the Levant – embody a principle of fertility which guarantees the survival – perhaps even the prosperity – of the group, by letting its agriculture flourish.

While the Hassuna and Samarra cultures developed side by side in northern Mesopotamia, another culture had emerged in the great flood plain of the lower Tigris and Euphrates. Although the newcomer showed some signs of contact with its northern cousins, the form it took was largely original. The Ubaid culture, as it is known, arose in an area of Lower Mesopotamia which had probably been inhabited for some time, though all trace of the earlier inhabitants has since disappeared due to silt deposited by the river and the rise in the groundwater level. Their successors were agricultural peoples. They probably grew cereals using elemen-

VASE
5th millennium BC, Iraq,
painted pottery with geometrical
design,
Ubaid 3 period,
height 16 cm (6 1/4 in).
Musée du Louvre, Paris.

FEMALE FIGURINE
5th millennium BC, Ur,
baked clay,
Ubaid culture,
15 cm (5 7/8 in).
British Museum, London.

**The stylised treatment of the face
gives this slim figure a characteristic
snake-like appearance.**

GOBLET
5th millennium BC, Iraq,
painted pottery with geometrical
design,
Ubaid 3 period,
height 13 cm (5 1/8 in).
Musée du Louvre, Paris.

tary irrigation techniques, and raised animals. These would have been mainly cattle, which were the species best adapted to this semi-aquatic environment of marshland and lakes which stretched across the deltas of the Tigris and the Euphrates as far as the lagoons along the Gulf coast.

The Ubaid culture lasted from the middle of the 7th millennium until the beginning of the 4th. There are six identifiable periods, Ubaid 0 to Ubaid 5. They can all be observed at the site of Tell el'Ueili, built at the heart of these former marshlands, which today are practically a desert.

The oldest level at Ueili that is still above groundwater level is defined as Ubaid 0. The first phase of this level, beginning around 6500 BC, contains the foundations of a vast granary, made up of low walls running parallel to one another or intersecting at an angle. The houses which must once have surrounded it have not been discovered. The existence of a granary for the collective storage of grain implies the communal management of resources based on networks of solidarity. In the next phases of Ubaid 0, substantial houses were found, built out of unbaked semi-moulded brick. As in northern Mesopotamia, or earlier in Syria, these houses are each divided into three parts. A large central hall where the household could foregather, its roof resting on two rows of posts, was flanked on either side by a series of smaller rooms, which served as either living rooms or storage areas. In one corner of the house was a staircase leading up two flights to the terraced roof. In one of these large houses, a small painted head with an elongated skull and "coffee bean" eyes was found. These characteristic traits can be found in all later Ubaid figurines.

The following period, Ubaid 1, appears to have begun about 5900 BC. The houses were built on the same plan as before, but the large granaries were now replaced by smaller structures where grains could be treated before storage. The greater number of such facilities would seem to indicate that the population was growing and that production was increasing, thus making it more difficult to find ways of managing resources collectively. As society evolved, so its mastery of the techniques of ceramics grew. Decoration was no longer just an ornamental device, it was also a means of social differentiation. Ubaid 0 and Ubaid 1 potters may have restricted their repertoire to geometrical patterns, that did not stop their design becoming ever more complex. During the Ubaid 2 period, which covered the second half of the 6th millennium, this trend continued: forms became more varied, the quality of both paste and painting improved, and the designs, while still geometrical, became extremely intricate. The Ubaid 2 culture, mainly known through its pottery, differed from its predecessors in that it began to spread out beyond the bounds of southern Mesopotamia into the central part of the region. Contacts were established with other nearby cultures – in particular with the ceramic cultures of the plains of Susiana and Deh Luran to the east, which were clearly influenced by Lower Mesopotamia, and with the Halaf culture that had recently supplanted the Samarra culture to the north.

The Halaf culture seems to have been imported from the Jezirah, and the people who brought it to northern Mesopotamia seem to have settled there over a period of time beginning in the early 6th millennium. They lived in small villages: each community would split once its population grew beyond a certain point, and so their villages multiplied rapidly. By the middle of the millennium, they had reached the Mediterranean coast to the west (Ras Shamra) and Lake Van (Tilki Tepe) to the north. To the south, they stretched as far as the valley of the Diyala. Halaf building was generally archaic in form, favouring small round houses, but its ceramic art was very advanced. These finely made objects were decorated with painted designs, first in brown and later in polychrome. Besides the traditional geometrical motifs, they also revived stylised versions of well-known Neolithic symbols, such as rosettes and bucranes. In the same revivalist manner, they made female figurines of painted baked clay, whose ample forms and squatting pose suggestive of the act of childbirth clearly relate them to the theme of fertility. Such practices would seem to relegate the Halaf culture to the domain of the past. Yet the vast geographical area it came to cover and its ever more intimate interaction with the Ubaid culture to the south place it firmly at the centre of the patterns of cultural and economic exchange that characterise the 6th millennium. The increasingly frequent use of seals impressed in clay to identify the ownership of merchandise is there as proof.

The emergence of the hierarchical society

The golden age of village society, based on egalitarian structures and collective co-operation, was already over by the end of the 6th millennium. A new form of social organisation was beginning to emerge, which was destined to flourish over the next two thousand years as trade assumed ever greater economic importance.

The Ubaid 3 period, which began around 5300 BC, already shows significant changes in architectural style which reflect this transformation. Change is most visible in the great monumental edifices that began to be erected, their grandeur emphasised by their being built on artificial terraces to raise their foundations above ground level. The first such building to be discovered was at Eridu (then located much nearer the Gulf), and had clearly been entirely rebuilt at each successive level of the site. It covers a surface area of about 130 square metres (1,400 square feet), divided into three parts. The huge central hall has a podium running along the main axis, with benches on either side. Many other smaller rooms give onto this central hall. The walls, with many openings, are made of unbaked brick, reinforced at intervals with pilasters.

The prestigious status of such buildings is obvious in both their monumental scale and their dominant position in the town. Yet there is no evidence that they had any religious function. They were much larger than all the other buildings, and were designed in such a way as to open onto the outside world. This suggests that they served as meeting places for the community. Many labourers would have been required to build them, and the organisation of the work points to the existence of a recognised centre of authority within the community – probably an individual, whose status and function would have been regularly reaffirmed by the practices and

rites for which the building was designed. With the appearance of such public structures, we move from a society based on interdependence among equals to one founded on relations of dependency. This was the first sign of greater inequalities to come.

Little is known about the domestic architecture of this period. The existence of grain stores, such as those at Ueili, shows that many traditional features of the agricultural economy had been preserved. In Lower Mesopotamia, flax and date palms were now cultivated alongside the usual cereals. There are many tools surviving from this period: stone hoes for working the soil, baked clay pestles and sickles. Ceramics, however, seem to have lost their function as a social marker, reverting to simpler designs and less elaborate methods of production.

This Recent Ubaid culture was destined to spread rapidly throughout the region. Its more highly structured forms of collective organisation made for a stable, yet dynamic, society. The Halaf communities in northern Mesopotamia were in regular contact with their southern neighbours, and by the end of the 6th millennium had adopted their culture. The result was a hybrid, known today as "Northern Ubaid". The northern culture was slow to follow its southern model when it came to changing its mode of organisation.

In the south, architecture and society continued to evolve at a smart pace. During Ubaid 4 (from 4700 to 4200 BC) and Ubaid 5 (from 4200 to 3700 BC), a profound transformation took place which was to lead, through a process of radical diversification, to the emergence of a truly complex society. At Eridu, as further north at Uruk and Tell Uqair, new monumental buildings were erected, on the same principles as those of Ubaid 3, but on an even larger scale. The height of the terraces increased and the surface area of the buildings reached 230 square metres (2,475 squares feet) at Eridu VII, and 280 square metres (3,010 squares feet) at the next level (referred to as Eridu VI). The walls were more substantial, the entrances more numerous, and the decoration more splendid. These changes were a direct response to the needs of an ever-growing population. There were more people to take part in the collective rituals, and slowly but surely these great buildings seem to have taken on a sacred aura. But they were not for all that temples in any strict sense of the term, and no religious objects have ever been found in any of them.

As the Ubaid culture drew to a close, its ceramics grew ever simpler, as production was standardised and accelerated. The resulting objects are characterised by their green paste and geometric or floral designs. The anthropomorphic baked clay figurines familiar from earlier Ubaid periods were still being made, and in even greater numbers, throughout southern Mesopotamia. Most of these figures represent women, and clearly belong to the tradition of the statuettes of Tell es-Sawwan; but their style is quite original. The body is slim, and stands upright. There is often a moulded clay decoration on the shoulders. The head has an elongated skull and "coffee-bean" eyes, which together give the figure a somewhat snake-like appearance.

Southern Mesopotamia had thus established itself as a veritable laboratory of social innovation. Wherever it led, the rest of the Near East was not long

BEAKER
4th millennium BC, Susa,
painted pottery,
Susa 1 period,
height 28.9 cm (11 3/8 in),
diameter 16.4 cm (6 1/2 in).
Musée du Louvre, Paris.

The pottery of this period is extremely well finished, with complex painted decorations. This beaker brings together three animal species native to the region: waders common in the marshes, saluki dogs from the desert and, below, a large mountain ibex.

BEAKER
Detail.

to follow, thanks to myriad networks through which ideas, as well as goods, were rapidly exchanged. In central Mesopotamia, the sites of Tell Abada and Tell Maddhur in the Hamrin mountains soon began to evolve towards a more hierarchical social structure. In northern Mesopotamia, the tripartite buildings organised around a large central hall at Tepe Gawra are very similar to those of Eridu. This region was an important crossroads for many major trading routes, and the use of personal seals to mark objects was common there too. The symbolic repertoire of such seals is mainly composed of animal figures, but also includes a distinctive human figure, known as the "master of the animals". Meanwhile, the Ubaid culture continued to extend its influence, as far as eastern Anatolia in the north, and the shores of the Gulf to the south. There trading relations were established with the local communities, and there is evidence that goods were transported along the coast by ship.

The first towns

During the Recent Ubaid period in southern Mesopotamia peasant villages, which had for millennia constituted the only known framework of human life, began to give way to larger settlements. In this new environment an elite class began to emerge, whose members enjoyed certain powers and privileges. They owed their wealth to the control they exercised over systems of trade and exchange. Yet this differentiation was not yet a full-blooded social hierarchy. This would only emerge in the following period, known as the Uruk period, which covered the best part of the 4th millennium. It was then that the villages of Lower Mesopotamia were transformed into genuinely urban centres.

The Uruk period is named after the site of Uruk, situated at the centre of the great Mesopotamian flood plain, on the banks of one of the branches of the Euphrates. Drainage and irrigation had begun to turn the surrounding marshes into extraordinarily fertile farmland, which could support a far more densely concentrated human population. During the 4th millennium, the site of Uruk grew by leaps and bounds. The first two phases of this process, Early Uruk (3700–3400 BC) and Middle Uruk (3400–3100 BC), are still not very well understood, especially regarding the evolution of their architecture. Overall, there is no evidence of a substantial break with the culture of earlier periods. Thus, the so-called "Cone-Mosaic Temple" which was found in level VI (*i. e.* at the end of the Middle Uruk) is still organised on the traditional tripartite plan. It is of modest size, rests on a limestone base, and is surrounded by limestone walls decorated with niches. The brick walls of the temple itself are decorated in an original manner, with a mosaic made out of small cones of different coloured stone; it is from this that the building derives its name. The innovative splendour of the temple suggests the prestige and wealth of the men who had it built. This recently-emergent ruling class benefited from the invention of new management tools, such as tokens used in accountancy, and maybe also personal seals in the form of small cylinders.

During this period ceramics were manufactured only for utilitarian ends, and gradually all attempt at decoration ceased, leaving only monochrome – grey or red – vessels. Simultaneously another kind of pottery was emerging, known to archaeologists as *Glockentöpfe*. These are small bowls with very thick sides and bevelled rims. They were made with no great care and in great quantity, which suggests they were mass produced. They have been found at many sites, from Anatolia as far afield as the eastern borders of the Iranian plateau, bearing witness to the Uruk culture's expansion of long-distance trade. This development was doubtless the result of southern Mesopotamia's growing need for wood for building, and for stone and minerals, all commodities which were unavailable locally. The Uruk culture thus came to spread widely throughout the Near East. Indeed, during the Middle Uruk period one might even speak of veritable colonies being established, at least in northern Syria (Habuba Kabira) and eastern Anatolia (Hassek Hüyük and Arslantepe). Elsewhere, Uruk settlements abroad were little more than trading posts, as at Godin Tepe and on the Iranian plateau. The same is true of Susa, which was founded around 4000 BC at the foot of the Zagros Mountains, and where we again find the familiar tripartite buildings standing on a raised terrace. Even Egypt seems to have fallen under the spell of the Uruk culture at this period, so all-embracing was its influence.

It was during the final stage of the Uruk culture, known as Late Uruk (from 3100 to 2900 BC), that the changes that had been working themselves out in Mesopotamian society since the Late Ubaid period finally came together to create a wholly new way of life and a wholly new form of social organisation. The result was the birth of the urban civilisation which is still, to a large extent, the civilisation we know today. The "town" of Uruk is the prototype of all towns to come – a gigantic conurbation spread over approximately 250 hectares (about 620 acres), with a population of between 30,000 and 50,000 inhabitants. Uruk's transformation into an urban centre seems to have been accomplished over a relatively short span of time. It was doubtless the result in part of its role as administrative centre of a vast and wealthy agricultural region, and in part of its fortunate situation on the banks of the Euphrates, at the heart of a substantial network of trade routes that had grown considerably in importance during the 4th millennium.

The city was organised around two official districts, which occupied substantial areas at its centre. To the west was the "White Temple", while to the east was the complex which would later be known as the Eanna. This impressive group of monumental buildings occupied a walled enclosure. There were several different levels to the site, and the scale of the buildings was considerable, with some measuring more than 80 metres (262 feet) in length. While the tripartite plan persists even here, there are also some innovative structures: a square building, an edifice with pillars, a monumental courtyard, and yet another building that constitutes a veritable labyrinth. New construction techniques were also in evidence, such as square bricks or artificial materials derived from gypsum. The walls are organised around a succession of niches and redans, or decorated with cone

Pages 42–43
TABLET WITH PICTOGRAPHIC WRITING
Late 4th millennium BC, Iraq, limestone,
4.5 x 4.3 cm (1 3/4 x 1 5/8 in).
Musée du Louvre, Paris.

This tablet is one of the oldest documents known in the history of accountancy. The surface is divided into compartments, in which are inscribed various pictographic signs, some of them representing numbers.

SPHERICAL ENVELOPE (BULLA) AND TOKENS
Late 4th millennium BC, Susa, lightly baked clay,
diameter of the bulla 6.5 cm (2 5/8 in).
Musée du Louvre, Paris.

These accounting tools predate the invention of writing. The tokens are of various forms, according to the number represented and the kind of product concerned. They are sealed inside spherical clay envelopes (*bullae*) for protection.

PRIEST-KING
Late 4th millennium BC, Iraq,
impression of a cylinder-seal,
height 6.2 cm (2 1/2 in).
Musée du Louvre, Paris.

The seal shows the priest-king accomplishing his ritual duties. He is assisted by a figure holding ears of wheat which will be fed to the sacred herd at the sanctuary of the goddess Inanna.

These statuettes use simple
volumes to great effect. They
show the priest-king naked,
doubtless in a ritual context.

STELE OF THE PRIEST-KING HUNTING LIONS
Detail.

mosaics in coloured stone or clay. The Eanna was traditionally interpreted as a group of temples. But closer examination reveals that the different edifices are not isolated buildings, but form a single complex architectural form. The complementary structures of the parts were completely integrated into a whole that was continuously being extended and revised. Its monumental scale, large courtyards and magnificent ornamentation, also suggests much more plausibly that this was a palace – in which case, it is the oldest known example of such a building.

What we know of the organisation of Uruk society also supports this hypothesis. The Eanna complex, separated from the rest of the city by its high walls, is the perfect illustration of the increasingly hierarchical nature of that society. Life in the new urban community was defined by the diversification of social functions and the specialisation of labour. The city being principally an economic and administrative centre, the majority of its population was no longer engaged in agricultural work. Instead, they relied on neighbouring towns and villages to supply them with food. The city was, above all, the seat of power. It was in the city that the need for an administrative system capable of managing both a diversified economy and a complex society would finally lead to the birth of that radical new reality – the State.

The cylinder-seal established itself as one of the distinctive signs of this emerging authority. It was probably invented as early as the Middle Uruk period, when it replaced the simple seal that had been widely used before, especially in northern Mesopotamia. These small stone cylinders could be engraved over their entire surface area. They served to impress the owner's mark into the clay seal of a container. The cylindrical form allows a larger surface to be printed more quickly, simply by rolling the seal across it, as well as the use of more complex motifs. The result is often a rich symbolic composition characteristic of the new social order, in which the representation of ritual scenes plays a prominent part.

But the decisive innovation was the invention of a system of communication which could guarantee rapid transmission of precise, reliable information. The different tools for counting and recording that had been devised previously had all proved to have their limits. Simple tokens were followed by *calculi* of various sorts for representing goods and quantities, to help businessmen memorise the details of their transactions. Later on, these devices were placed inside clay *bullae* to ensure they would not be interfered with, and a cylinder-seal was used to prove that the record had in fact survived intact. Gradually, the practice emerged of recording the results of the transaction on the outside of the *bullae*, using notches, so that the seal did not have to be broken every time the contents were referred to. In due course, the *bullae* were dismissed as a useless complication, and replaced by a simple clay tablet, which was easier to handle. It was on this tablet that writing made its first appearance. Combining notches (numerical values) and pictographic signs (representing an object or an idea), the result was a juxtaposition of symbols which did not as yet refer explicitly to an underlying language. Some of the pictographs are simple and easy to decipher, while others, which are more complex, are still not understood by archaeologists. Yet from the moment of its first appearance, writing appears to constitute a fully functioning semantic system, which reveals no trace of the great intellectual struggle, which must have led to its birth.

About five thousand documents were found on the site of Uruk, most of them financial and economic. Whether accounting records of agricultural production, lists of herds or goods, or texts dealing with the administration of lands or the employment of labourers, they all point to the existence of long-established methods of management. Other documents constitute first steps towards a theoretical organisation of the world, and of the new social order that was then emerging. Lists and classifications are drawn up, in which concepts are grouped and ordered by categories. One enumerates the titles and names of the main professions, placing them in a hierarchical order. At the apex of the social pyramid is a figure whose title will later come to mean "king", followed by the chiefs of the different groups of priests, and then the artisans.

Official iconography confirms the existence of an exceptional individual, who is always depicted according to a well-established set of conventions. This repertoire includes not only images on glyptics, but also a new monumental art. The small figurines of the Neolithic period have given way to

STELE OF THE PRIEST-KING HUNTING LIONS

Detail. Late 4th millennium BC,
Iraq,
basalt,
height 78 cm (30 5/8 in).
Iraq Museum, Baghdad.

FEMALE MASK

Late 4th millennium BC,
Uruk,
white limestone,
height 20.1 cm (7 7/8 in).
Iraq Museum, Baghdad.

a much more imposing sculptural project, both in relief and in the round. In all these works, the chief figure is portrayed realistically, as a bearded man wearing a headband or perhaps a cap, and a long skirt, when he is not simply naked. These images doubtless had a ritual significance. The figure is shown winning victories over his enemies, hunting big game or presiding over communal ceremonies. All these different activities were later associated with sovereignty, whence the name of "priest-king" that has traditionally been attributed to this figure. Surrounded by a privileged elite and commanding an administration that now possessed the power of writing, the sovereign is the incarnation of the new social order. In the civilised space of the town, a new world – hierarchical in nature and monarchical in its politics – was in the process of being born.

2. Cities

During the second half of the 4th millennium, the great flood plain of southern Mesopotamia was the scene of a decisive transformation in human society – the emergence of towns. Several urban centres developed along the branches of the Euphrates and the Tigris, and beside the main canals of the irrigation system. These cities expanded at a steady pace. Uruk, for example, already occupied 500 hectares (1,235 acres) by the beginning of the 3rd millennium – an area larger than that of 5th-century Athens or Rome under Augustus. In the towns, different peoples met and mingled, yet they all to some extent shared in a common culture – that of the Sumerians, the inventors of the art of writing.

Who were these Sumerians[1]? Their language belongs to no known linguistic group. The continuity of the archaeological evidence that has been found on the major sites of Lower Mesopotamia, from the Ubaid period onwards, suggests that they were the descendants of a people who had been established there, if not since their very origins, then certainly for an extremely long time. Yet the names of the great rivers and major towns of the region are not Sumerian, nor even Semitic. This would seem to point to the existence of another quite distinct ethnic group already established in the area prior to the Sumerians' arrival. In that case, the Sumerians would be foreigners who arrived in Mesopotamia during the 4th millennium – like the Akkadians, who spoke an eastern Semitic language. The latter seems to have come from the north-west, having migrated down the Euphrates into Lower Mesopotamia. It was the meeting of such diverse populations that led to the profound cultural symbiosis that underpins Mesopotamian civilisation.

SANCTUARY KNOWN AS THE SACRED ENCLOSURE
Mid-3rd millennium BC.
Palace of Zimri-Lim, Mari, Syria.

Passageway leading from the cella to the central hall.

FEATHERED FIGURE
Archaic Sumerian Dynasties, Telloh (formerly Girsu), white limestone, *18 x 16 cm (7 x 6 1/4 in).*
Musée du Louvre, Paris.

This figure is reminiscent of the priest-king of the Uruk period. He stands at the entrance to a sanctuary, represented by the two staffs.

Pages 52–53
THE SACRED JOURNEY OF THE GOD EA
Detail. Akkadian Dynasty, Iraq, impression of a cylinder-seal, *height 2.7 cm (1 in).*
Musée du Louvre, Paris.

In Mesopotamian mythology, Ea is the god of fresh water, which brings fertility to the land.

1. The name "Sumer", like the term "Sumerian" which is derived from it, comes from the Akkadian word *shumeru*, which was used in the 3rd millennium to refer to the southern part of Lower Mesopotamia. The northern part was called Akkad, and its inhabitants Akkadians. The Sumerians however, in their spoken language, referred to their land as, simply, *kalam*, meaning "the country". In writing, they called it *ki.en.gi*, that is, "the country that is master of the reed".

GROUP OF FIGURES PRAYING

Archaic Sumerian Dynasties,
Tell Asmar (formerly Eshnunna),
gypsum,
*heights between 23 and 72 cm
(9 and 28 3/8 in).*
Oriental Institute of Art, Chicago.

WOMAN WEARING A POLOS

Circa 2400 BC, Mari,
gypsum,
height 14.8 cm (5 3/4 in).
Musée du Louvre, Paris.

**This tall head-dress was probably
worn by priestesses.**

The city-states of Sumer (2900–2330 BC)

During the first half of the 3rd millennium, the Sumerian lands were divided between a series of small monarchical states. Each state was centred on one or more towns, its territory barely extending beyond those towns' agricultural hinterland. The most southern of these city-states gave onto the marshy coastline of the Gulf[1]: among them was the important religious centre of Eridu, dedicated to Enki, the god of fresh water and its fertility-bringing powers. A little further north lay Ur, the great metropolis of the region and a port whose wealth depended on the maritime trade that ran between the Euphrates and the Gulf. The heartland of Sumer was dominated by the cities of Uruk and Larsa to the west. In the east lay the state of Lagash and Girsu (known today as Telloh), which was locked in continuous conflict with its neighbour, Umma. Further to the north again, the most important town was the holy city of Nippur, home to the great temple of the god Enlil, "the King of all the lands", which was later to play a crucial role in legitimating certain Sumerian rulers' pretensions to hegemony. To judge by the names they left behind, ethnic Sumerians seem to have occupied some 80% of the land of Sumer. In the less heavily urbanised civilisation of Akkad, to the north of Nippur, Semitic Akkadians were in the majority. Their main city was Kish, situated at a point of great strategic importance where the courses of the Euphrates and the Tigris draw close together. There it was able to control the trade routes to the north, which brought wood and minerals to Sumer and along which Sumerian culture was disseminated to other peoples. On the Tigris, the town of Ashur (or Assur) was an important staging post and benefited greatly from this Sumerian influence. The Subir (known today as the plain of Jezirah) to the west of the Tigris was likewise strewn with small urban communities, which were organised into networks around a few larger cities, such as Tell Brak (probably the Nagar of Antiquity) or Tell Khuaira.

Trade with the north-west was also the reason behind the foundation of Mari on the Euphrates, probably as early as the 29th century BC. Lying midway between Lower Mesopotamia and Syria, the city occupied a privileged position which allowed it to control the flow of traffic through the valley. River-borne trade would seem to have been made easier by the building of a canal between the Euphrates and its tributary the Habur. Abandoned at one point for almost a century, Mari was reoccupied and the town, which had been rebuilt in the Mesopotamian style, was soon flourishing again. Further to the north, in the Syrian interior, the city of Ebla enjoyed an equally brilliant development, thanks above all to its situation at the crossroads of the trade routes which linked the valley of the Euphrates to the east, the Anatolian plateau to the north, and the Mediterranean coast to the south-west, where the harbour of Byblos (Gubla in the local Semitic language) maintained warm relations with that great commercial and political power, Egypt. Evidence of this intimacy can be found in stone vases marked with the cartouche of the Old Kingdom Pharaohs, Khafre and Pepy I, which were presented as gifts to the ruler of Ebla. The

1. The Arab-Persian Gulf was Mesopotamia's main outlet to the sea. At that time, it was known as the "Lower Sea", in opposition to the "Upper Sea", *i.e.*, the Mediterranean.

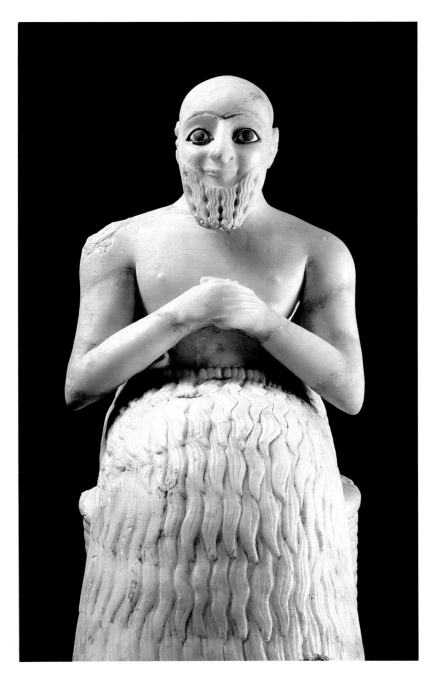

WOMAN WEARING A POLOS

Detail. Circa 2400 BC, Mari,
gypsum,
height 14.8 cm (5 3/4 in).
Musée du Louvre, Paris.

| Left
STATUE OF EBIH-IL

| Circa 2400 BC, Mari,
alabaster,
height 52.5 cm (20 5/8 in).
| Musée du Louvre, Paris.

This statue represents a high official
of Mari. It is dedicated to the goddess Ishtar. The eyes are made of
encrusted shell and lapis lazuli.

| Right
MAN AT PRAYER

| Archaic Sumerian Dynasties,
Tell Asmar (formerly Eshnunna),
gypsum,
height 72 cm (28 3/8 in).
| Iraq Museum, Baghdad.

This is the largest of a group of
votive statues that were found
buried beneath the Temple Square.

THE ROYAL STANDARD OF UR
Archaic Sumerian Dynasties, Ur,
double mosaic panel of shell,
red limestone and lapis lazuli,
height 20.3 cm (8 in).
British Museum, London.

The upper panel – "Peace" –
represents a ceremonial banquet
presided over by the king. The
lower panel – "War" – depicts the
victorious king of Ur leading his
army back from battle.

Pages 62–63
THE ROYAL STANDARD OF UR
Detail of the "War" panel.

people of Ebla, like those of Mari, for the most part used a Semitic language[1], but lived alongside other ethnic groups who predated their arrival, just as in Lower Mesopotamia.

The second major axis of Mesopotamian trade ran east towards Iran. Its royal road was along the valley of the Diyala, the Tigris' main tributary, which provided the best way into the fastness of the Zagros Mountains. Wealthy cities such as Eshnunna and Tutub (now known as Khafaji) soon sprang up at the entrance to the valley, bringing the Sumerian culture with them. Another route ran further to the south, leading to the plain of Susiana (known to the Sumerians as Elam, "the High Country"), which was a sort of Mesopotamian outpost at the foot of the Iranian plateau. Its urban centre was Susa, founded over a thousand years previously. Its culture alternated between periods of strong Sumerian influence and periods of great originality, when its main point of reference was Iran. By the end of the 3rd millennium, the area was largely under the sway of an autonomous regional culture known as proto-Elamite, which had its own system of writing, probably inspired by the Sumerian script. This culture petered out around 2700 BC, and Susa was once again assimilated into the Sumerian sphere of influence.

Although they were many, the city-states of Mesopotamia seem all to have had a similar institutional structure. The territory of each was administered, in the name of the city's god, by a ruler who was that god's repre-

1. The language of Mari, together with the Akkadian language, makes up the linguistic group known as eastern Semitic. The language of Ebla is the oldest known example of a western Semitic language.

sentative among men. At this period, the ruler bore one of three titles. *En,* "the lord", had a religious connotation – the first documented usage was at Uruk in the proto-urban period, where it was related to the function of the priest-king. *Lugal,* on the other hand, meant literally "the great man", and was perhaps first applied to military leaders. *Ensi,* the most "neutral" of the three, at first had the meaning of "prince", and later "governor".

The legitimacy of royal power rested on a privileged relationship to the divine. Yet the monarchy was also keen to establish its independence from the temple. It was to this end that palaces were built in every city, as symbols of this emerging secular power. The brick architecture so characteristic of Mesopotamia reached a new level of achievement in these monumental edifices – for instance, in the two palaces at Kish, the one at Eridu and the one at Eshnunna. Palace A at Kish, which is only partly excavated, is a good example of the official architecture of the period. A monumental entrance hall gives onto an open square, around which two main buildings house the reception rooms and their annexes. The royal apartments themselves were probably located on the first floor. Large palaces were also built in the northern cities, at Mari and at Ebla. At the same time, most towns were surrounded by fortified walls, as protection against marauding nomads or (more commonly) in case of conflict between neighbours.

Although the palace had begun to lay claim to a central position in Mesopotamian life, the great temples were still important foci, not only of

religious and cultural authority, but of economic power too, thanks to the huge estates which were managed by the *sanga*[1]. At Khafaji, the main temple was designed on the model of a citadel, surrounded by a double oval wall. The outer wall enclosed the entrance courtyard, along one side of which ran a substantial accommodation block, which was probably home to the temple staff. The inner wall opened onto a second courtyard, around which were ranged various storehouses and other buildings, and which led to the sanctuary proper, which stood on a raised terrace. Only serving priests and the king himself were admitted to this inner sanctum.

Although no statue or image of a god has ever been found in the various temples that have been excavated, we know from texts that they were displayed there. However, many statues have been found in these holy places representing human figures – members of the royal family, dignitaries, priests and scribes. Some female figures have also survived, who for the most part seem to represent priestesses. These statues were placed in the temples as a sign of perpetual and silent worship. Figured in attitudes of prayer, they make up a portrait gallery whose manner evolves over the course of the period from stereotyped beginnings to a more realistic style towards the end. The figures found in the square temple at Eshnunna, their angular bodies dominated by extraordinarily large encrusted eyes, are

PERFORATED WALL PLAQUE

Mid-3rd millennium BC,
temple of Ninhursag, Susa,
alabaster,
14 x 13 cm (5 1/2 x 5 1/8 in).
Musée du Louvre, Paris.

The ritual banquet was seen as the supreme expression of civilised life and of man's mastery over the forces of nature.

1. The Sumerian term *sanga*, which is the origin of the Akkadian *shangu*, referred to "the administrative director of the temple", who was also responsible for the organisation of its rites.

in sharp contrast to the sculptures associated with Mari, such as the figure of the scribe Ebih-Il, which exude instead a sense of delicacy and serenity. The temples were also decorated with small votive stone plaques, which were fixed to the walls through a hole in their centre. Carved in relief, the designs are often organised into two registers depicting complementary themes: the world of nature in the lower register, featuring animals that were either hunted or mastered; and the world of divine ceremony in the upper register, whether ritual banquets or offerings to the gods – the founding acts of the civilised world. This fundamental dialectic between nature and culture summarises in a single composition the intrinsic order of the world.

A similar symbolic structure underlies the organisation of what is generally known as the "Royal Standard of Ur", and of the corresponding (and incomplete) piece from Mari. This double composition on the themes of peace and war uses the motif of the procession to present a large number of figures, fashioned in shell and fixed in bitumen on a double wooden panel, against a background of red limestone and lapis lazuli. The standard was among the sumptuous burial goods found in a 26th-century necropolis. This burial ground stood at the centre of Ur, close to the temple of the moon-god Nanna, the tutelary deity of the city. It contained over a thousand tombs, of which fifteen were genuinely monumental constructions, with either a vaulted chamber or a shaft, in stone or brick, reached via an access ramp. Three of these tombs, to judge by the cylinder-seals placed in them, were the final resting places of King Meskalamdug, his queen, Pu-Abi, and King Akalamdug. In the larger tombs, several people, or even several dozen people, were all buried together: soldiers, servants and courtesans would thus accompany their ruler or their lord in death. If these were human sacrifices – which is far from certain – then they are the only known example of this practice in Mesopotamian history.

The civilisation of Ur is rich in objects which testify to the high level of craftsmanship and technology, particularly in metalworking, achieved during the 3rd millennium. This culture was in part made possible by the development of long-distance trade, bringing gold, silver and copper from the mountains of Anatolia, tin (which together with copper was needed to make bronze) from the borders of the Iranian plateau, lapis lazuli from Afghanistan and red limestone from India. The emerging oligarchy's need to assert its prestige was an important stimulus, and also led to significant exchanges in the cultural domain. The Sumerian story of the former king of Uruk, Enmerkar, alludes to this ambitious and far-ranging commercial activity. Enmerkar followed the example of his father, Meskiangasher, who had "entered into the sea and scaled the mountains", thus enlarging the horizon of Sumer. Having built the ramparts of Uruk, his son decided to embellish the temples of his city, for which he required access to such prestigious commodities as gold, silver, lapis lazuli and red limestone. He demanded the submission of the king of the land of Aratta, which was separated from Sumer by seven mountains, and which was doubtless situated somewhere on the Iranian plateau. This demand led to negotiations, which required frequent journeys to be made by emissaries carrying messages between the two kings. According to the myth, it was in order to

VOTIVE MACE HEAD OF MESILIM
Archaic Sumerian Dynasties,
Telloh (formerly Girsu),
speckled breccia,
height 19 cm (7 1/2 in),
diameter 16 cm (6 1/4 in).
Musée du Louvre, Paris.

This emblem of the power of the Sumerian king is decorated with a picture of a lion-headed eagle clutching in its claws a frieze of six lions.

VOTIVE MACE HEAD OF MESILIM
Detail.

guarantee the accuracy of these messages and compensate for the lapses of human memory that Enmerkar invented the art of writing on clay tablets. In fact, writing predated the reign of Enmerkar by several centuries. The first surviving examples date from around 3300 BC at Uruk. But the beginning of the 3rd millennium saw an evolution away from pictographs and towards a phonetic script, using signs which are known now as cuneiform[1]. Inscribed texts were produced in ever-increasing numbers. They were principally business documents, yet among them are a few literary texts (hymns to temples, anthologies of wise sayings and some mythological narratives), which can now only be read with difficulty, due to the highly archaic nature of the language. There are also a large number of royal inscriptions, essentially brief dedications engraved on votive objects that were to be placed in the temples of the major gods. These documents are uneven in quality and limited in nature, yet they provide a decisive insight into the lives of some of the rulers of the main city-states during the first two thirds of the 3rd millennium, the period which is known today as that of the "archaic dynasties".

The oldest of these inscriptions concerns a king of Kish, Mebaragesi, whose name figures on fragments of a vase dating from the 27th century BC. This evidence corroborates the indications to be found in the

---

1. Cuneiform script was derived from the earlier pictographs, whose linear outlines were replaced by a series of indentations in the form of a nail or wedge (*cuneus* in Latin), whence their name.

"Sumerian King List", a document that was drawn up in the early 2nd millennium, according to which Mebaragesi "carried off as booty the weapons of Elam". His son Agga, once he had been crowned king in his turn, declared war against Gilgamesh, king of Uruk, who was the third in order of Enmerkar's successors. The king list states: "Kish was conquered: kingship was carried away to Eanna [= Uruk]". Gilgamesh, at first merely a great ruler, was later promoted to mythical status as the hero of the most important epic cycle in Mesopotamian literature. Throughout the century that followed, it was the kings of Ur who dominated the politics of Sumer. During the first fifty years, these monarchs were buried in the great necropolis at the centre of their city. Then, from 2550 BC onwards, the town was ruled by Mesanepada and his successors, who together constitute the First Dynasty of Ur. It was at this period too that a king of Kish by the name of Mesilim extended his authority south as far as Adab and Lagash, intervening to settle a conflict between the latter and its neighbour Umma. The state of Lagash, which was controlled for a while by Mesilim, occupied the south-eastern part of Sumer, from the Tigris in the west to the shores of the Gulf, where it had established a port. It was situated where the road from Susa and the Iranian plateau reached Mesopotamia, and it was this location which was the foundation of its wealth, even if it also had to suffer occasional raids by the Elamites as a consequence. Around 2500 BC, the *ensi* Ur-Nanshe founded at Lagash what is easily the best documented dynasty of the archaic period. Ur-Nanshe's role as founder, and in particular as builder or restorer of the great temples of the city, is celebrated on a number of votive plaques decorated with reliefs of ceremonial scenes. On the largest of these plaques, the king is depicted carrying a hod of bricks and presiding over a ritual banquet, surrounded by his family and various dignitaries. The inscription alludes to the city's trade with Dilmun, a country centred on Bahrain that included many of the islands of the Gulf, and whose ships supplied Sumer with wood for building as well as with many luxury goods.

Throughout the First Dynasty, the history of Lagash is dominated by a recurring conflict with the neighbouring city of Umma. At a moment when the balance of power had swung against Lagash, Eannatum, the grandson of Ur-Nanshe, who reigned around 2450 BC, led a successful military campaign against the enemy, decimating their army, and restoring the earlier border between the two states. On the mound that marked this frontier, he erected a victory stele, known as the "Stele of the Vultures", on which he was depicted marching at the head of the army under the protection of his tutelary god Ningirsu. The inscription declares: "May the man of Umma never cross the frontier that is Ningirsu's. May he never alter its mound and its ditch. May he never move its stele. If he should cross the frontier, may the great net of Enlil, king of heaven and earth, on which he has sworn, fall upon Umma!" The victory over Umma served as a prelude to other military successes, against the cities of Uruk and Ur, against Elam and (possibly) Mari. Under Eannatum, the power of Lagash was at its greatest. Yet the curse that was inscribed for all eternity on the Stele of the Vultures was unable to prevent the renewal of hostilities. Despite Entemena's vic-

STELE OF THE VULTURES
Detail of the mythological side.

The enemies vanquished by Eannatum are caught in the great net of the god Enlil.

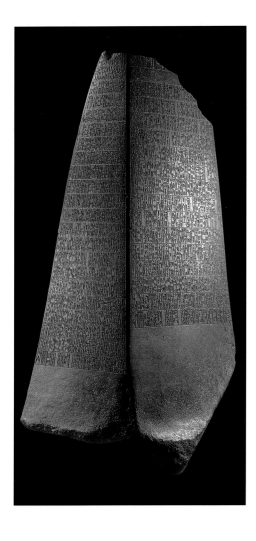

tories around 2400 BC and the "fraternal treaty" he signed with the king of Uruk, Lagash had already entered upon an irreversible decline. A usurper known as Uruinimgina attempted to prevent any further loss of influence by promoting an ambitious policy of administrative and social reform. His edicts are recorded on a series of clay cones[1]. But his reforming zeal arrived too late. Lagash was overrun around 2340 BC by Lugalzagesi, king of Umma, who, having taken control of the principal towns of Sumer, had himself consecrated "King of the Land" at the holy city of Nippur: "When the god Enlil, the King of all the lands, had given Lugalzagesi kingship over the land, [...] when he had subjugated all the countries from where the sun rises to where it sets, then from the Lower Sea by the Tigris and the Euphrates as far as the Upper Sea, he made all the ways safe. From where the sun rises to where it sets, the lands lived in peace, and the peoples irrigated the land joyfully."

The Akkadian empire (2334–2193 BC)

When Lugalzagesi united the great cities of southern Mesopotamia under a single central authority at the end of the 24th century BC, it marked the beginning of a process of unification that was henceforth ineluctable. The traditional form of political organisation, founded on the model of the city-state, was increasingly inappropriate. It led to an administrative fragmentation which was unable to cope with the spiralling demand for raw materials brought on by a combination of demographic and economic expansion. More direct control over sources of essential supplies was required, especially given the distances involved. Wood and minerals are entirely lacking in Mesopotamia, and had to be brought in from the mountains of the Levant and Anatolia or from the southern shores of the Gulf.

It was control over the trading routes with the North that was the origin of Ebla's wealth, as well as the privileged relations it enjoyed with the other great Semitic cities of Mari and Kish. As a result, an independent culture began to develop there, though one that still retained many characteristic Mesopotamian features. Both Ebla and Mari adopted the cuneiform script to transcribe their local languages. The royal palace of Ebla, where the king lived surrounded by thousands of courtiers and servants, was not simply the political and economic centre of the state, but also housed an important written archive. From this we know that in the 24th century BC, during the reigns of Igrish-Halam, Irkab-Damu and, above all, Ish'ar-Damu, Ebla was the capital of a powerful state which dominated the entire region as far as the Euphrates, and which constituted an ever greater threat to Mesopotamian trade.

Increasing competition with Ebla was a major factor influencing the emergence of a centralised political structure in Lower Mesopotamia. Lugalzagesi's state may have enjoyed only a brief hegemony over the region, but his defeat at the hands of the Akkadian monarch Sargon, far from undermining the project of unification, only accelerated the establishment of a new political framework. The age of the city-states was well and truly over.

1. This is the oldest known instance of the practice of royal promulgation of "legislation".

Little is known about Sargon's origins. According to a much later tradition, he was the child, by an illicit affair, of a high priestess, who placed him in a basket and cast him adrift on the Euphrates, much in the manner of the Moses of the Bible. Rescued and raised by a gardener, he was appointed cup-bearer[1] to the king of Kish, the great metropolis of the land of Akkad, where the majority of the population spoke Semitic languages. Sargon[2] subsequently left Kish to found his own capital, which was known as Akkad (or Agade)[3]. His victory over Lugalzagesi, who was led in chains to the door of the temple of Enlil at Nippur, gave him control over the whole of southern Mesopotamia. He thus assumed the title of "King of the Land", in addition to "King of Akkad" and "King of Kish". In order to strengthen his hold on power, he had the walls of the great cities of Sumer razed to the ground, and in them he installed various "sons of Akkad" as governors (*ensi*), along with his own administrators and garrisons.

Sargon's political and military ambitions were not limited to Lower Mesopotamia. He soon turned his attention to northern Syria, a key trading zone, whose roads looked increasingly vulnerable to the growing power of Ebla. One of Sargon's inscriptions records his conquest of this region: "Sargon bowed down in prayer at Tuttul before the god Dagan. [Dagan]

VICTORY STELE

Akkadian Dynasty,
Telloh (formerly Girsu),
limestone,
34.5 x 28.5 cm
(13 5/8 x 11 1/4 in).
Musée du Louvre, Paris.

1. A prestigious position in the royal courts of the ancient Near East.
2. The name Sargon itself, which is the biblical form of the Akkadian *Sharrum-kin*, meaning "legitimate king", is a sign *a contrario* of the fact that he was a usurper.
3. The location of the city of Akkad is still unknown. It seems likely that it was situated in the region of Baghdad.

gave him the Upper Country, [with] Mari, Yarmuth, Ebla, as far as the Forest of Cedars and the Mountains of Silver[1]." His authority stretched as far as the Jezirah, as is shown by the Akkadian archives found at Tell Brak (formerly Nagar), which was the region's political centre. His influence even appears to have reached as far afield as the Anatolian plateau, where he intervened to help a colony of Mesopotamian merchants residing in the city of Purushanda when their safety was threatened by a local conflict. To the south-east, Sargon was able to dominate Susa and the land of Elam, thus controlling the essential trade routes serving the Iranian plateau and central Asia. Indeed, ships came from even further afield – from Meluhha (the valley of the Indus), Magan (Oman) and Dilmun (Bahrain and the islands of the Gulf) – bearing luxury goods to the "quays of Akkad".

One royal inscription gives some measure of the extent of Akkad's military power: "To Sargon, King of the Land, the god Enlil gave him no rival. Enlil gave Sargon the Upper Sea [the Mediterranean] and the Lower Sea [the Gulf]... Mari and Elam stood before Sargon, the King of the Land." Even if such claims did not always translate into permanent control of territory, especially in the more distant regions, the very scale of this kingdom required the new king, if he was to have some chance of holding on to

1. The site of the city of Tuttul is known today as Tell Bi'ah. It is close to the junction of the Euphrates and the Balih. The "Forest of Cedars" and the "Mountains of Silver" are probably a reference to the Amanus Mountains in Syria and the Taurus in Anatolia, both of which are rich in wood and minerals.

CYLINDER-SEAL AND IMPRESSION

Akkadian Dynasty,
Mesopotamia,
green jasper,
height 2.7 cm (1 1/8 in).
Musée du Louvre, Paris.

The scene depicts the sacred
journey of the god Ea.

what had been achieved, to establish a much more centralised state than any that had been seen so far. Thus the powers of the king were extended, and the loyalty of his agents was bought with land that had either been purchased or confiscated. Henceforward, the relationship of the people to the monarch was explicitly represented as one of personal dependency.

Yet Sargon did try to preserve some of the Sumerian institutions, even as he brought them under his own control. He appointed one of his own daughters high priestess of the god Nanna at Ur, where she took the Sumerian name of Enheduanna. Tradition has it that she was a celebrated poet, and the author of many religious hymns, including a series in honour of the goddess Inanna. Sumerian culture thus survived in part, but the language was wholly replaced in administrative documents by Akkadian (at that time, Old Akkadian), even in the southern cities. Writing, weights and measures were all standardised. For the first time, Mesopotamia was governed as a single entity, but its unity was fragile. The old Sumerian cities did not readily accept this new authority which had swept away many of their traditions. By the end of Sargon's reign, revolts had begun to break out. Under his two sons, who succeeded him, they would become an ever more frequent occurrence.

Rimush, who mounted the throne on his father's death in 2278 BC, was thus confronted with uprisings in several cities in Sumer, and in particu-

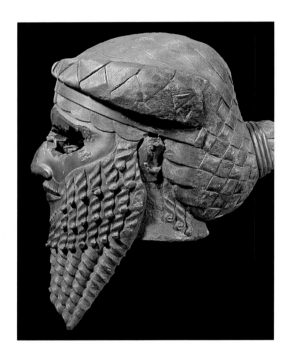

**HEAD OF A KING,
POSSIBLY NARAM-SIN**
Akkadian Dynasty, Nineveh,
copper,
height 36.6 cm (14 3/8 in).
Iraq Museum, Baghdad.

**HEAD OF A KING,
POSSIBLY NARAM-SIN**
Detail.

lar in Ur and Lagash. He successfully repressed them, and also waged victorious campaigns against the kingdoms of the Iranian plateau, re-establishing Akkadian control over Elam and returning home with substantial spoils of gold, copper and slaves. Manishtushu succeeded Rimush in 2269 BC. He continued his brother's military exploits, pushing even deeper into the Iranian plateau and sending his fleet across the Lower Sea as far as the "mines of silver" and the sources of the black diorite[1] in which he had his own monumental statues sculpted. It was under Sargon that the royal workshops had begun to produce the kind of large-scale sculpture appropriate to the ideology of the new political system. Victory stelae and life-size statues of the king explicitly conspired to glorify the new rulers.

Cylinder-seals had been a privileged form of artistic expression since the beginnings of the urban era. During the Akkadian period this art reached its apotheosis. In these mythological translations of nature, all the principal gods were represented, accompanied now by their symbolic attributes (streams, flames, weapons or branches). At the same time, political unification led to the construction of a unified pantheon, bringing together the different local gods, once tutelary spirits of the various cities, and organising them into a hierarchical vision of the world.

When Manishtushu's son, Naram-Sin, inherited the throne in 2254 BC, he set about converting the kingdom of Akkad into a veritable empire. He started by consolidating Akkadian hegemony through a series of military campaigns. One of these took him into northern Syria, where he sacked the cities of Ebla and Armanum, and proclaimed himself master "of the land of Elam as far as Marhashi, and of the land of Subartu as far as the Forest of Cedars". However his reign, like those of his predecessors, was troubled by repeated uprisings in the larger cities. One general revolt even required nine successive battles to be waged before order could be restored. Nor was the irredentism of the cities of Sumer the only threat to the stability of the Akkadian state. The semi-nomadic populations that lived along the borders of the empire were rapidly becoming a major problem. This was particularly true of the Amorites, who lived in the steppes to the west of the Euphrates and spoke a Semitic language, and of the Guti and Lullubi who inhabited the central Zagros Mountains to the east.

The famous victory stele of Naram-Sin commemorates the defeat of Satuni, king of the Lullubi. The composition, striking for its unity, shows the triumphant sovereign leading his troops through wooded mountains. The naturalistic treatment of landscape along with realism in depicting human figures had already begun to emerge in the art of Naram-Sin's predecessors. By the time of the victory stele, however, these conventions have evolved into something very different from those of the archaic period. This work is also notable as the first recorded depiction of astral symbols. They hang in the sky, as Naram-Sin seems to advance towards them in his horned cap, an emblem traditionally reserved for the gods.

Written documents also bear witness to the deification of Naram-Sin during his lifetime. Scribes would use the sign indicating divinity before his

1. The "mines of silver" have not been identified. Diorite came mainly from the mountains of Oman, which was known at that time as the Land of Magan (or Makan).

name. He is called the "god of Akkad", and oaths are sworn by his name. The nature of power itself changed, and the Akkadian monarchy was proclaimed to be divine in origin. It was thus necessarily universal, extending as by right to the very frontier of the civilised world. This is the significance of the new royal title adopted by Naram-Sin, "King of the Four Regions" – that is, of the whole world.

However, Akkad's pretensions to universal power did not last long. Naram-Sin's son, Shar-kali-sharri, who succeeded to the throne in 2217 BC, was forced to abandon them in the face of mounting pressure from the Amorites and the Guti. All the territories that had been subjugated over the preceding century and a half were lost, and the Akkadian dynasty only managed to survive for a few more decades by withdrawing into its capital city. Yet the new conception of sovereignty that had evolved would fare better than the state where it was born. Henceforth the Akkadian empire was the model that all future Mesopotamian rulers would seek to emulate.

The Third Dynasty of Ur (2112–2004 BC)

After the Akkadian empire collapsed, the Guti, who had dealt the final blow, proved unable to establish anything more than theoretical control over the Mesopotamian plains. The great cities of the south had suffered less at their hands than had Akkad itself, and were soon able to escape their control. Lagash was one of the first Sumerian states to regain its independence. A new dynasty emerged there around 2150 BC, which led to a revival of Sumerian culture, beginning with the restoration of the traditional temples.

This trend was reinforced with the coronation of Gudea in 2125 BC. Girsu then apparently became the capital of Lagash: the king resided there, as did his administration. Gudea used a combination of formal alliances and informal influence to control relations with the other cities of Sumer. He consolidated the wealth of his state by reviving the long-distance trade routes. Wood and stone began to arrive again from the Gulf and from Syria, providing the materials for a major reconstruction programme. Fifteen or so temples were restored, foremost among which was the Eninnu, the great sanctuary of the tutelary deity Ningirsu. An extensive account of this decision[1], which was inspired by the gods, and the ritual execution of the divine will that followed, has been preserved in cuneiform inscription on a series of large clay cylinders. When the sanctuary was finished, it constituted a veritable complex of sacred buildings and spaces. There was a solemn ritual, observed by the great divinities of the Sumerian pantheon, to celebrate the entrance of the god, accompanied by his servants, into his house. Then, "respect for the temple filled the whole country; the fear it inspired took hold of the foreigner; the dazzling light of Eninnu covered the universe like a cloak".

Gudea was a deeply pious man. His name means, literally, "the Chosen One". He engaged in an on-going conversation with the gods of his city, through the many statues of himself which he dedicated in their temples. They were sculpted in the royal workshops, usually in diorite that was

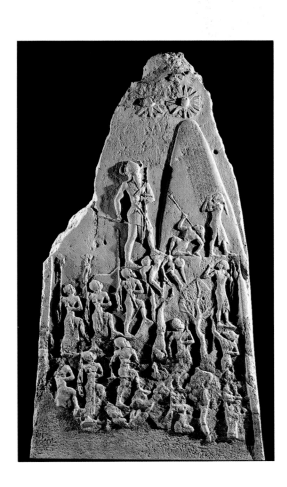

1. These are the longest surviving texts in the Sumerian language.

brought from the distant land of Magan. They show the king with his hands joined in prayer. Many of them celebrate the founding acts of the state. These functions, which are an emanation of the divine powers, are the prerogative of the ruler. He is seen as the builder of the city, in particular of the major public and religious buildings, and thus as the architect who organises the space of urban civilisation. Even more fundamentally, the king is identified as the "nourisher" of his people, the master of the waters, bringing fertility, and thus prosperity, to the land.

Despite the brilliance of Gudea's reign, the state of Lagash did not long survive his death. However, the other cities of Sumer had meanwhile embarked on a similar process of self-renewal, centred on the revival of their traditional cultures. In 2116 BC, Utu-hegal, king of Uruk, led a general revolt that threw off the shackles of Guti dominance. Tirigan, king of the Guti, "prostrated himself at the feet of Utu-hegal. [Utu-hegal] placed his foot on [Tirigan's] neck... Royalty was restored to Sumer".

The ruler of Uruk thus became master of all of Lower Mesopotamia. But in 2112 BC, he was overthrown by Ur-Nammu, who may have been his son, and whom he had personally appointed as *shagin* (military governor) at Ur. Having founded the Third Dynasty of Ur, Ur-Nammu had himself proclaimed "King of Sumer and Akkad" at Nippur. In doing so, he assumed for himself and for his successors the political heritage of the Akkadian empire, while at the same time restoring the primacy of the Sumerian language and culture. Peace and prosperity returned to the country under the protection of the gods of Sumer. Ur-Nammu diligently restored their temples and erected colossal tiered towers, known as ziggurats, beside them. Justice was standardised throughout the empire, through the promulgation of the oldest known anthology of exemplary judgements to be produced in Mesopotamia, "Ur-Nammu's Code". This document was probably compiled during the reign of his son, Shulgi. Under the Code, the poor man, the widow and the orphan were to be protected from the powerful. As the sovereign stated in the prologue: "I will not deliver up the man who owns only a sheep to the mercy of the man who owns an ox."

Ur was once again a major trading port, now without rival in the region. The city was redesigned by Ur-Nammu, with a large canal running right through it and broad avenues to either side. The ramparts were rebuilt, beside the Euphrates on the west. Many temples of different sizes were scattered across the town. At its centre was the sacred precinct, which was built on a vast terrace. This was the site of the palace known as E-hursag ("Mountain-House"). Close by was a group of imposing religious buildings, including the temple of Nanna, the city's tutelary god, and the Giparku, which served as the residence of his high priestess. The sacred precinct was dominated by a ziggurat made up of three raised terraces, one on top of the other. The terraces were reached by a massive staircase in three flights, which led to the temple at the top. Like all monumental Mesopotamian architecture, this impressive edifice was built out of bricks laid in regular courses and held together with bitumen.

The city of Ur and the empire which it sought to revive reached their peak during the long reign of Shulgi, who succeeded Ur-Nammu in 2094 BC.

STATUE OF GUDEA, WITHOUT INSCRIPTION
Detail. Second Dynasty of Lagash, Telloh (formerly Girsu), diorite, *height 107 cm (42 1/8 in).* Musée du Louvre, Paris.

STATUE OF GUDEA SITTING
Second Dynasty of Lagash, Telloh (formerly Girsu), diorite, *height 46 cm (18 1/8 in).* Musée du Louvre, Paris.

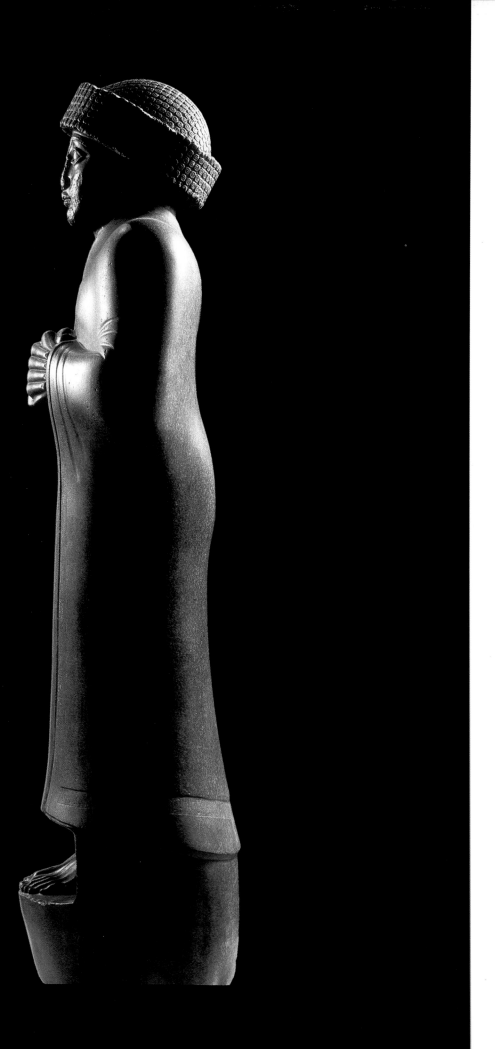

| Left
STATUE OF GUDEA WITH
OVERFLOWING VASE
| Second Dynasty of Lagash,
| Telloh (formerly Girsu),
| calcite,
| *height 62 cm (24 3/8 in).*
| Musée du Louvre, Paris.

| Centre and right
STATUE OF GUDEA,
WITHOUT INSCRIPTION
| Second Dynasty of Lagash,
| Telloh (formerly Girsu),
| diorite,
| *height 107 cm (42 1/8 in).*
| Musée du Louvre, Paris.

During his first years as king, he concentrated on consolidating his power and continuing the programme of urban reconstruction begun by his father. In the eighteenth year of his reign, however, Shulgi established a standing army, and embarked on an ambitious series of military and diplomatic campaigns. He was able in particular to extend the frontiers of his empire as far as Ashur and Urbilum (Arbela) in the north, which were later to be the heartland of the Assyrian state, and Susa in the east.

The great Elamite city of Susa at the foot of the Iranian plateau had already been drawn into the Sumerian sphere of influence during the archaic period. As a result, it had come to adopt the Sumerian culture and with it cuneiform writing. It then fell into the hands of Akkad, until that empire in its turn collapsed. Thereupon Susa was annexed by the last ruler of an Elamite Dynasty known as the Awan Dynasty, which had managed to maintain an independent power base deep in the Zagros Mountains. This king, Puzur-Inshushinak, was a contemporary of Ur-Nammu. He introduced a new form of writing, known as linear Elamite, alongside the Akkadian cuneiform already practised in Susa, thus bearing witness to the bilingual nature of its population. Under his rule, the city resumed its lucrative role as a trading centre at the crossroads between Mesopotamia and the Iranian plateau. Goods could be found there from as far afield as the Indus Valley, where the Harappean civilisation – which also possessed its own form of writing – was then at its peak. As well as all these advantages, however, Susa also suffered one major disadvantage: its location at the point of arrival of the tin roads gave it a strategic importance which made it an obvious target for the revived Sumerian power in Ur. Shulgi soon captured Susa, and then set about protecting his new eastern frontier by forming alliances with a series of Iranian states.

The empire of Ur was now almost as vast as had been that of the kings of Akkad. In the interests of stability, Shulgi established a centralised administration, creating countless registry offices which kept a close eye on every aspect of economic activity. Large centres were also created for the collection and redistribution of the goods that were given to the state in payment of taxes[1]. These centres each specialised in a particular category of goods: for example, that at Puzrish-Dagan received payments in the form of cattle, and was responsible for making sure that temples, civil servants and members of the royal household all received exactly the amount due to them. Major towns had their own *ensi* or governor, who was generally a member of the local royal family. Each governor was closely supervised by a *shagin* or military commander, who reported directly to the ruler of Ur. The system was underpinned by a remarkably sophisticated communications network, with numerous staging posts at the disposition of the royal messenger corps.

This work of centralisation created a great deal of economic activity in its wake, and both were recorded in legal and financial documents inscribed on countless tablets. The resulting archives imply a considerable increase in the number of scribes. They also testify to an impressive harmonisation of the calendar – which until then was different in each city – as well as of

1. There were two main taxes at this time: *bala*, paid monthly by the central provinces of the empire, the lands of Sumer and Akkad, and *gun mada*, which was paid by the outlying regions.

scribal practices through the development of a writing-based education system. It was this which in turn made possible the unification of the many different cultural legacies which the state of Ur had inherited with its empire. This was also one of the golden ages of Sumerian literature, dominated by the composition of hymns in honour of the great gods, and also of the king. Like Naram-Sin before him, Shulgi, himself a man of letters, chose to organise his own deification while he was still alive, as a mark of the supreme power he had achieved.

When his forty-eight-year reign came to an end, Shulgi left behind him an empire whose organisation was in many ways exemplary, and which seemed to have a long period of stability ahead of it, even though external threats to its security were on the rise. The extraordinary prosperity of the people of Ur naturally attracted the envy of those who lived outside its frontiers: the Elamites to the east, the Hurrians to the north and the Amorites to the west. The temptation must have been increased by the fact that the rest of the Near East was at that time in a state of general crisis. This external pressure mounted steadily throughout the reigns of Shulgi's two sons. Amar-Sin was the first to succeed his father, followed in 2037 BC

STELE OF UR-NAMMU
Detail.
Third Dynasty of Ur,
Ur,
limestone,
width 105 cm (41 3/8 in).
Iraq Museum, Baghdad.

The king offers a libation
to the moon-god.

by his brother Shu-Sin. They each had to deal with regular raiding parties, and sometimes with full-blooded military assaults. To contain the Amorites, a wall was even built between the Tigris and the Euphrates at the point where their courses are closest to each other.

With the accession of Ibbi-Sin, son of Shu-Sin, in 2028 BC, the empire's days were numbered. The power of the king of Ur was shrinking steadily with each year, as the larger cities reclaimed their independence one by one. By the tenth year of his reign, Ibbi-Sin's effective control had been reduced to the city of Ur itself and its immediate surrounding territory. However, while Ur was in decline, a confederation of small principalities had been put together in the Zagros Mountains towards the middle of the century. Known now as the Kingdom of Shimashki, its rise was nothing short of meteoric. Anshan on the plateau, and then Susa, were rapidly integrated into its empire. Kindattu, king of Shimashki and Elam, was thus in a position to take advantage of the chaos in Mesopotamia. He invaded the flood plain and laid siege to the city of Ur in 2004 BC, which soon fell to the Elamites. Ur was sacked and its last ruler, Ibbi-Sin, was led away in captivity to die in the distant city of Anshan.

Ashur and the Amorite kingdoms (2004–1792 BC)

While Mesopotamian society had evolved over the course of the 3rd millennium towards a unified imperial state, those parts of the Levant situated between Palestine (the ancient land of Canaan) and northern Syria were still, in organisational terms, at the stage of the city-state. This region was inhabited by peoples who mostly spoke western Semitic languages. They built their cities on hill tops, as a rule, and surrounded them with ramparts. This was particularly true of Canaan, where sites such as Megiddo, Tell el Farah (formerly Samaria), Ai and Tell Yarmuth were protected by substantial fortifications. At Yarmuth, the elements of a palace complex have been identified. Imperial Egypt was the essential economic horizon of these cities; not only did the Pharaonic state control the mines of nearby Sinai, but it even had military outposts within Canaan itself.

Egypt was also engaged in commercial relations with the great port of Byblos, located further to the north on a promontory which formed two naturally protected harbours. This trade included cedar wood, resins that were needed for the process of mummification, olive oil and wine. Byblos also did business with Syria, in particular with Ebla, and probably as far

ZIGGURAT OF UR

Third Dynasty of Ur.
Ur, Iraq.

The great staircase
leading to the first of
the three terraces.

afield as Mesopotamia as well. It was a wealthy city, with its palace complex and its religious monuments, foremost amongst which was the sanctuary of the tutelary goddess worshipped under the name of Ba'alat Gebal, "Lady of Byblos". Ba'alat Gebal's reputation spread as far as Egypt, where she was identified with the goddess Hathor. Yet in Byblos, as in Canaan, the authorities made no use of writing, despite the volume of trade in which they were involved.

After 2300 BC, the whole of the Levant suffered a decline whose causes are only obscurely understood. There would seem to have been a combination of ecological and economic factors. Trade in particular fell off, partly due to the decline and then fall of the Old Kingdom in Egypt. In any case, urban civilisation was in retreat for the rest of the millennium; many cities were abandoned, and some were destroyed. This wave of destruction which spread across Palestine and into Syria is generally linked by historians to the migration into the area of Amorite tribes, though this hypothesis is far from certain. The Amorites took their name from "Amurru", which is the Akkadian word for "west". They first appear in the archives of Mesopotamia during the reign of Naram-Sin, when they were already perceived as a mounting threat to the state. Their rapid penetration of Mesopotamia went hand in hand with the disintegration of the empire of Ur under its last ruler, Ibbi-Sin, during the final years of the 3rd millennium.

Each of the great cities that were now left to themselves soon developed a local dynasty, leading to a thorough fragmentation of Mesopotamian power. In many cases, it was Amorite chiefs who took control, which would seem to indicate that they were already well integrated into what was in any case an increasingly Semitic society, where the main spoken language was Akkadian. Amorite itself never became a written language, and its speakers rapidly found themselves assimilated into the traditional culture of Mesopotamia.

The most powerful of these new dynasties was founded at Isin in 2017 BC by Ishbi-Erra, a Semite who came from Mari. Appointed governor of northern Sumer by Ibbi-Sin, he gradually established his power independently of Ur. Although the territory they ruled over was more modest in its dimensions, the kings of Isin saw themselves as continuing the tradition of the former empire, even assuming the title of "King of Sumer and Akkad". Sumerian slowly fell out of use as a spoken language, to become exclusively the language of men of letters and priests. It was at this time that most of the great works of Sumerian literature were written down or copied out in

their definitive form. The "Sumerian King List" was also established at this time, with the aim of presenting the new dynasty in a glorious context of thousands of years of Mesopotamian rule. The *de facto* supremacy of the city of Isin over the rest of Lower Mesopotamia reached its apotheosis with its fifth king, Lipit-Ishtar (1934–1924 BC). It was during his reign that the Enigsisa – "the House of Justice" – was built, and a legal "code" was promulgated, directly inspired by the Code of Ur-Nammu; it was to be one of the last great texts written in Sumerian.

Towards the end of his reign, Lipit-Ishtar found himself confronted by the expansion of another Sumerian city, Larsa, situated further to the south. It was governed by an Amorite dynasty, whose fifth king, Gungunum (1932–1906 BC) was a formidable warrior. His military campaigns led him as far as Elam, where the Shimashki dynasty had given way in the 20th century BC to the rule of the Sukkalmah, or "Grand Regents", who reigned simultaneously over both Anshan and Susa. Closer to home, Gungunum proceeded to deprive the king of Isin of control of the city of Ur, whose port was still the key to the Gulf trade. As a result, Larsa went on to enjoy a period of great prosperity, as is evident in the magnificence of the religious complex of E-Babbar – the "Radiant House" of the sun-god Shamash. However, Gungunum's successors were only able to preserve their hegemony over Lower Mesopotamia by waging perpetual wars against their rivals in Isin. In 1834 BC Kudur-Mabuk, an Elamite ruler from Emutbal, east of the Tigris, took advantage of this situation to place his son, Warad-Sin, on the throne of Larsa. Warad-Sin was succeeded by his brother Rim-Sin (1822–1763 BC) whose long reign saw the final flowering of the economy and culture of Sumer, thanks in part to the unification of the kingdoms of Larsa and Isin after the latter fell to its rivals in 1794 BC.

In northern Mesopotamia, an independent dynasty of local origin had emerged at the beginning of the 20th century BC in the city of Ashur. Built on a rocky promontory overlooking the valley of the Tigris, at the entrance to a region of fertile foothills sheltered by the natural ramparts of the Zagros Mountains, Ashur had been an important staging post on one of the major trade roads linking Mesopotamia with Syria and Anatolia since the beginning of the 3rd millennium. As a result, it had been incorporated into the empires of both Akkad and, later, Ur. Its first steps towards becoming an independent dynasty seem to have been due to one Puzur-Ashur, whose name, like those of his immediate successors, is Akkadian. The rare surviving cuneiform inscriptions that refer to these early years illustrate the development of the Assyrian language, which was then little more than a dialect of Old Akkadian. The first kings of Assyria founded their power on privileged relations with the priests of the city-god Ashur, presenting themselves as the priests' *ishiakkum*[1] – their "lieutenant". This nascent political and cultural authority was associated with a revival of commercial activity largely organised by the rulers of Assyria themselves. It was King Erishum I, for instance, who pronounced "the freedom of silver, gold, copper, tin, barley and wool" during the latter half of the 20th century BC. Thanks to such new legislation, the great families of

1. The Assyrian title *ishiakkum* is derived from the former Sumerian title *ensi*.

PECTORAL DECORATED WITH A FALCON
Early 2nd millennium BC,
Byblos, imitation of an Egyptian
design,
gold and silver,
12 x 20.5 cm (4 3/4 x 8 in).
Musée du Louvre, Paris.

PECTORAL DECORATED WITH A FALCON
Detail.

Pages 92–93
CAPPADOCIAN TABLET
Detail. Late 20th century BC,
Kanesh,
clay,
height 6.3 cm (2 1/2 in).
Musée du Louvre, Paris.

The cuneiform text records a
decision by the judges of the
karum of Kanesh.

Ashur were able to develop a vast network of trading posts, chiefly along the roads leading to Anatolia.

The Anatolian plateau too, like other parts of the Near East, had seen the emergence of city-states in the course of the 3rd millennium. Each of these city-states was organised around a fortified town, and was governed by a "prince", who was considered a "great prince" if he managed to bring several such cities under his control. All relied heavily on the vast quantities of minerals buried in the surrounding mountains for their wealth. Metalworking techniques reached an extraordinary pitch of perfection in the region, as can be seen in the burial goods that have been found in the royal necropolises, for example at Alaça Hüyük.

The abundance of copper in Anatolia meant that the production of bronze[1] became an important activity. But local resources of tin were soon exhausted, and this rare mineral had to be imported from the other end of the Middle East – the mountainous regions bordering the Iranian plateau. Due to its central position on this route, Mesopotamia was the natural intermediary in the tin trade, and Mesopotamian merchants had established offices in Purushanda, at the heart of Anatolia, as early as Sargon's reign. The benefits of this trade were felt throughout the whole of the high plateau of central Anatolia, which was inhabited by a people known as the Hattians. Cities such as Kanesh and Hattusa grew wealthy on its proceeds. Trade between Anatolia and Mesopotamia was briefly interrupted by the period of political crisis at the end of the 3rd millennium, but was soon re-established. Assyrian merchants took the initiative in this revival, setting up a complex system based on trading posts known as *karum* (or *wabartum*, if they were only minor offices) in the principal cities along the caravan routes. These donkey caravans would leave Ashur twice a year, laden with tin from the east and materials woven in Lower Mesopotamia. They would return from Anatolia bearing silver and gold, precious metals which were already universally recognised as a form of money. Cargoes and transactions were grouped together under the authority of the *karum* of Kanesh, to which all the others were subordinate. These trading posts constituted a separate quarter of the city where they were installed, most often in the lower town, in accordance with regulations called "oaths" agreed between the merchants and the local rulers. There the Assyrians could live according to their own customs, though relations with the local population were generally cordial, and intermarriage was certainly not unknown. Substantial cuneiform archives were built up, recording the details of their transactions. It is through these records and accounts that writing was introduced into Anatolia.

Towards the end of the 19th century BC, however, violent conflicts broke out across the region, and the Assyrian trading posts were brutally destroyed. Ashur's authority was weakened as a result, and the state fell into the hands of foreign invaders: first Naram-Sin, the ruler of Eshnunna, then Shamsi-Adad, the son of an Amorite chief from the middle Euphrates.

1. Bronze is an alloy containing approximately 90% copper and 10% tin. Arsenic had been used in place of tin up to the beginning of the 3rd millennium, but had proved too dangerous to handle during the production process.

Hammurabi and the rise of Babylon (1792–1595 BC)

The whole of the Near East had been adversely affected, though to different degrees, by the general political crisis that marked the end of the 3rd millennium. However, a measure of genuine prosperity soon returned, as a vast trading network based on the complementarity of economies and resources was painstakingly reconstructed. Politically, the result was still far from a reunification. Indeed, the great Mesopotamian empires were effectively replaced by a mosaic of small kingdoms, constantly at loggerheads with one another. Culturally, however, there was a definite tendency towards ever greater unity. Cuneiform writing was now practised universally, and Akkadian was recognised everywhere as the language of diplomacy.

In this new Near East, the Levant was to play a pivotal role, thanks to its location at the point of intersection of so many trade routes. The revival of Egypt under the Middle Kingdom only reinforced the strategic importance of its position, as the towns of the Mediterranean coast benefited more than most from the re-establishment of relations with Egypt. Byblos in particular saw its former glory restored. New sanctuaries were built, such as the "Temple of the Obelisks". Standing on a raised terrace, it took its name from the betyls in the sacrificial courtyard that led to its entrance. The hypogea of the royal necropolis contained some splendid burial goods, among whose treasures were jewellery and precious wares made in Egypt, as well as locally-produced objects which showed a strong Egyptian influence. Further north, the city of Ugarit[1], located near the coast at the entrance to a fertile plain, was also enjoying a revival of its fortunes. Its market places were a meeting point for merchants from all four corners of the known world, including Minoan Crete, where a palace culture similar in certain ways to that of the Near East was flourishing at that time. Such distant contacts are also a sign of the progress that had been made in maritime navigation.

The installation of Amorite dynasties in most of the major cities of the Levant, as well as in many Mesopotamian towns, only added to the intensification of commercial and cultural exchanges between them. Not only Ugarit, but the cities of inland Syria as well, such as Qatna and Aleppo – the capital of the Yamhad kingdom which had supplanted Ebla as the regional metropolis – were all ruled by kings of Amorite origin. So was Mari, which had regained its independence under the so-called Shakkanakku[2] dynasty after the fall of the Akkadian empire, only to be captured by Iakhdun-Lim, son of the chief of an Amorite tribe from the middle Euphrates, at the end of the 19th century BC. Mari thus became, for the space of two decades, the capital of a powerful kingdom that dominated the surrounding region as far as the Balikh river. However, barely two years after the death of Iakhdun-Lim, the city fell to a new Amorite conqueror. This second foreign ruler went by the name of Shamsi-Adad. Like Iakhdun-Lim, Shamsi-Adad was the son of the chief of an Amorite tribe from the middle Euphrates, who had become king of Ekallatum, a town on the Tigris to the north of Ashur. Having succeeded his father, however, Shamsi-Adad was driven out of Ekallatum by Naram-Sin, king of Eshnunna. After taking refuge for a while in the city of Babylon in central Mesopotamia, he reconquered Ekallatum, and then went on to capture Ashur, over which he was to reign for the next thirty-three years. From this position of strength, he came to control not only Mari, but the whole of northern Mesopotamia. He installed his elder son, Ishme-Dagan, at Ekallatum, and his younger son, Yasmah-Adad, at Mari, to guard over the two extremities of this huge kingdom. He himself established his capital at the centre of the northern plain, in a town he renamed Shubat-Enlil, "the home of the god Enlil". He thus placed his reign under the protection of the great Sumerian master god, from whom all power was held ultimately to derive. To the west, he entered into alliances with the main Syrian rulers, and re-established trading posts in the cities of Anatolia. At the end of this process, Shamsi-Adad was thus able to proclaim himself *Shar Kishati*, "the king of the whole".

This attempt to create a universal state, however, again failed to survive the death of its founder. His son Ishme-Dagan was unable to hold out long against the king of Elam, whose armies had soon destroyed Eshnunna, ravaged Assyria and captured Shubat-Enlil. Meanwhile on the Euphrates, Mari had been retaken by Zimri-Lim, a nephew of Iakhdun-Lim, with the aid of the king of Aleppo. There he reigned for fifteen years, until Mari fell to Hammurabi, king of Babylon. As for Assyria, it had been laid utterly waste, and would not recover from this blow for the best part of four centuries.

1. The city of Ugarit stood on the site of Ras Shamra, which had been inhabited since the 8th millennium.
2. The title Shakkanakku, literally "the governors", is derived from the term *shagin* which was used to refer to military governors under the Third Dynasty of Ur.

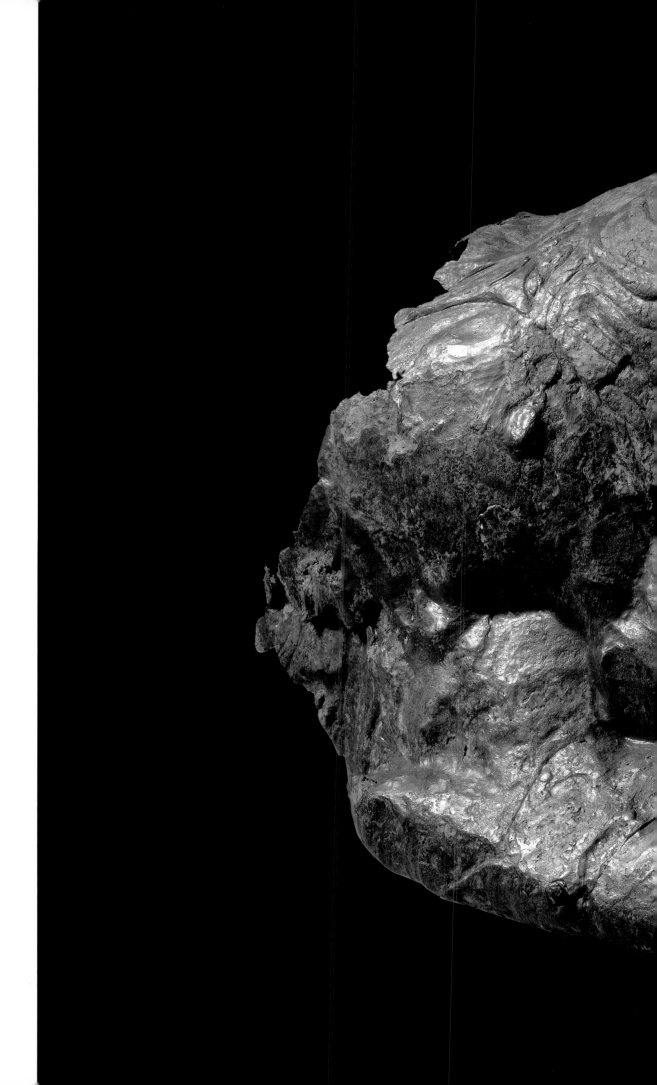

However, further to the south, a new power was emerging in Babylon. This city was located at the strategic heart of central Mesopotamia, a position which had already played a crucial role in the glory of Kish and Akkad during the previous millennium. It is indeed in documents dating from the Akkadian empire that the name of Babylon first appears, though it was then only a small town of no great importance on the east bank of the Euphrates. Yet, by the 21st century BC, it had been elevated to the rank of provincial capital with its own governor, under the Third Dynasty of Ur. In 1894 BC it was captured along with many other cities by an Amorite chief called Sumu-abum, who founded his own independent dynasty there. During his reign, and those of his first successors, the new kingdom did not however expand beyond the boundaries of the ancient land of Akkad.

The accession to the throne of Babylon in 1792 BC of the fifth king of this dynasty, Hammurabi, was not initially marked by any great changes. The early years of his reign were devoted to consolidating his power, and only a few small pieces of territory were annexed to the kingdom. "The man of Babylon" was above all prudent, and made sure that relations with "the great king" of Upper Mesopotamia, Shamsi-Adad, remained cordial. But on the latter's death the empire he had assembled began to break up, and the way was open for ambitious men to take advantage. Through a mixture of diplomatic strategy and military operations, Hammurabi began to take new areas of land under his control. He defeated the army of Elam, then secured his northern frontier through an alliance with Zimri-Lim, the king of Mari. This enabled him, in 1763 BC, to lay siege to the great southern metropolis of Larsa, which fell to his troops after several months' resistance, thus putting an end to the long reign of Rim-Sin. Having thus achieved a dominant position in southern Mesopotamia, he began to extend his power to the north. In 1760 BC he took Mari and burned it to the ground. In 1755, it was Eshnunna's turn to capitulate, and with it the whole of the eastern bank of the Tigris. By then, Hammurabi was the undisputed master of a new Mesopotamian empire, a worthy successor to Akkad and the Third Dynasty of Ur. On this basis, he felt entitled to revive the illustrious title of "King of Sumer and Akkad, King of the Four Regions". Henceforth, the heart of the empire was Babylon, which was not only the political capital, but also the religious and cultural centre. The city of the god Marduk thus replaced Nippur, the home of Enlil, as heir to the traditions of Sumer and Akkad. The legitimacy of royal power was still seen to be based on divine will. But now the king's authority was felt in every aspect of the life of society, thanks to an administration whose hierarchy was answerable to him alone. The palace was also the institution in which economic power was concentrated, besides which the state also encouraged a flourishing private sector in the domains of agriculture, craft and trade. In order to regulate the workings of an ever more complex society, Hammurabi had a new legal code drawn up. Modelled on the codes of Ur-Nammu and Lipit-Ishtar, but written in the Babylonian language, a local variant of Akkadian, its purpose was to "proclaim law throughout the land, eliminate what is bad or perverse, and prevent the strong from oppressing the weak". It was inscribed on a series of monumental stelae, so

that (according to the text itself) anyone would be able to have the articles relevant to their case read out to them. Two hundred and eighty-two exemplary situations are described, concerning which the king's decision had already been sought, and which cover all the main aspects of life in society. The sentence pronounced in each case is intended henceforth to serve as legal precedent.

The great kingdom of Hammurabi was only able with great difficulty to impose its administrative structures on the lands it had conquered. It was the creation of an exceptional man, and proved unable to survive his death. No sooner had his son, Samsu-Iluna, inherited the throne in 1749 BC than a severe economic crisis provoked revolts in many cities. Babylon lost control of southern Mesopotamia, whose towns were soon almost deserted. The whole region was in a state of crisis: the Gulf trade had been brough to a halt by the collapse of the civilisation of the Indus Valley on which it had depended. Henceforth the kings of Babylon ruled over an area reduced to central Mesopotamia and the middle Euphrates as far as Terqa, and the state they governed had been irremediably weakened. Groups of a people called the Kassites began to descend from the Zagros Mountains and settle on its territory. In 1595 BC the Hittite king, Murshili I, came down from the Anatolian plateau to conquer Aleppo, and his subsequent raid along the Euphrates dealt the Hammurabi dynasty its final blow. The next king of Babylon was a Kassite chief by the name of Agum-Kakrime, and his reign marked the beginning of a whole new era.

3. Peoples and empires

While the Amorites were taking control of the main cities of Mesopotamia and Syria, other peoples had been migrating into the lands to the north. Despite their diverse origins, these populations were gradually assimilated into the cultural world of the Near East, where they were to become major political forces. The Hurrians had lived on the mountainous northern border of Mesopotamia for a long time, and around 2100 BC founded several small independent states there. The most important of these was Urkish (known today as Tell Mozan), which was the centre of the cult of their principal god, Kumarbi. Although their language was quite distinct from all others spoken at this time, this would not prevent groups of Hurrians from settling in many of the cities of northern Mesopotamia and Syria over the coming centuries.

Several groups speaking an Indo-European language, whose dialects were all related to one another, had moved into Anatolia by the end of the 3rd millennium. The Hittites made their home on the high central plateau, while the Luwians settled in the southern part of the peninsula and the Palaites in the north-west. The kings of Kushar made a first unsuccessful attempt to bring central Anatolia under a single political authority in the 18th century BC, but it was left to a Hittite ruler to make this dream a reality, around 1650 BC. He established his capital in the town of Hattusas, which is located on a kind of natural citadel at the centre of the plateau. It was from the city that he took his name – Hattusilis, "the man from Hattusas". Hattusilis then

Pages 106–107

THE ISHTAR GATE

Detail of the front wall, reign of Nebuchadnezzar II, Babylon, glazed brick,

Vorderasiatisches Museum, Berlin.

FOUNDATION NAIL

Circa 2100 BC, Tell Mozan (formerly Urkish), bronze and limestone, *12.2 x 8.5 cm (4 3/4 x 3 3/8 in).*

Musée du Louvre, Paris.

This nail in the form of a lion protects the oldest known cuneiform inscription in the Hurrian language.

THE LION GATE

Neo-Hittite empire, outer walls of Hattusas.

Hattusas, Turkey.

The lions protect the gate that led to the upper town, which was the temple quarter of the Hittite capital.

STATUE OF KING IDRIMI
Early 15th century BC, Tell
Atchana (formerly Alalakh),
limestone and basalt,
height 103.5 cm (40 3/4 in).
British Museum, London.

**PENDANT REPRESENTING
A HITTITE GOD**
Neo-Hittite empire, Yozgat,
gold,
height 3.8 cm (1 1/2 in).
Musée du Louvre, Paris.

This type of figurine was worn as a
pendant in order to obtain the protection of the god or goddess represented.

tried to take control of the main road south, which would have given him
access to the great international trade routes. He first conquered the plains
of Cilicia, then advanced into Syria, where he took several towns. The conquest of Syria was only completed by his successor, Mursilis I, who captured
the regional capital of Aleppo. In a move of great strategic audacity, Mursilis I then pushed on to the Euphrates, as far south as Babylon. A major
power had emerged from the Anatolian highlands.

The emergence of new peoples (1595–1365 BC)

The taking of Babylon by Mursilis I in 1595 BC marked the end of the
Amorite dynasty which had ruled there for three centuries. Once again, a
foreign dynasty violently took control of the city. However, while a Kassite
aristocracy had soon filled the key political and military posts, the administration of the kingdom was left essentially in the hands of the
Babylonians. Moreover the Kassites, like their Amorite predecessors, were
themselves rapidly assimilated into the culture of Babylon, to which they
brought new dynamism. It was under their reign that the major texts of the
Mesopotamian tradition were collected and fixed in their definitive form.
Ancient sanctuaries were restored and new ones built. Thus King Kara-
indash, who ruled around 1415 BC, built a small temple in the religious
quarter of Uruk dedicated to the goddess Inanna. It was decorated with a
frieze in moulded baked brick which depicted a series of gods and goddesses carrying vases overflowing with water – a motif that is clearly
Mesopotamian. In the 14th century BC, a new royal city was founded close
to the northern frontier of the realm – and to the kingdom of Assyria,
which was then undergoing a revival. It was called Dur Kurigalzu, "the
fortress of Kurigalzu", in honour of the Kassite king who ordered it to be
built. It was organised around a huge palace and a temple overshadowed by
a great ziggurat. Babylon, however, remained the principal religious and
cultural centre, where the priests of Marduk were soon to succeed in estab-
lishing their god at the apex of the Mesopotamian pantheon. Marduk's
newly-acquired primacy was celebrated in the mythological narrative of
Enuma Elish, which was written down in the 12th century BC:

> *"Marduk, king of the gods,*
> *His realm is rich, and he himself is unchanging,*
> *His word endures and his command cannot be altered:*
> *No god can change what his mouth has uttered."*

While the Kassite kings were seeking to perpetuate the grandeur of Babylon
with the help of Marduk, the Hurrian principalities to the north came together in the course of the 16th century BC to create the state of Mitanni.
The population of this new kingdom was for the most part Hurrian, but
it was governed by an aristocracy of Indo-European origin. Expanding rapidly, its frontiers soon stretched as far as the Zagros to one side, and the
Mediterranean to the other. To the east Ashur fell under its influence, though
in Syria it met with a rival in the search for regional hegemony in the form

of the restored Egyptian empire. In the 15th century BC, the Pharaohs of
the 18th Dynasty hoped to take direct control of the wealth of the Levant.
Under Thutmose III, the Egyptian armies advanced as far as the Euphrates.
But the two rivals chose to enter into an alliance and share control of the
region. In this way, they were better able to withstand a new menace that
had emerged in the north, with the renaissance of the Hittite empire.
Around 1370 BC, a forceful leader called Shuppiluliuma acceded to the
throne of Hattusas. Having rebuilt the military power of the Hittites, he
took advantage of the weakness of Egypt under the reforming Pharaoh
Akhenaten to seize northern Syria in three campaigns from the Mitanni
king, Tushratta. The Mitanni state soon collapsed, undermined by dynastic conflicts. Meanwhile, under the rule of Ashuruballit I who ascended the
throne in 1365 BC, Assyria had at long last regained its independence.

The rise of Assyria (1365–934 BC)

The reign of Ashuruballit I (1365–1330 BC) marked the beginning of the re-
newed political and military ascendancy of Assyria. The new ruler conquered
part of Mitanni, established diplomatic relations with the Pharaoh of Egypt,
and even intervened in Babylon to settle a dynastic dispute. Assyria's rise to
power accelerated the decline of the southern city, which was suffering from
the fall-off in the Gulf trade, even if business with Egypt had to some extent

ROCK SANCTUARY

13th century BC.
Yazilikaya, Turkey.

The reliefs represent a
procession of gods from the
Hittite pantheon.

filled the gap. Under the reigns of Adadnirari I (1307–1275 BC) and
Shalmaneser I (1274–1245 BC), Assyria completed its annexation of the
Mitanni lands, thus gaining control over the trade routes to Syria and
Anatolia. An Assyrian administration was installed to supervise them, under
an appointed governor. Part of the local population was moved by force, and
their lands given to Assyrians. Under the banner of the god Ashur, who was
now portrayed as a warrior, a veritable empire was beginning to take shape.
To the west, the struggle for control of the Levant had resumed, this time between Hittites and Egyptians. Sety I and Rameses II, the great Pharaohs of the
19th Dynasty, pursued an expansionist strategy in Asia, and their armies regularly skirmished along the frontier of Syria. At the battle of Qadesh, circa
1285 BC, the Hittite king, Muwatallis II had managed to halt Rameses II's
progress. But Hattusilis III preferred to sign a treaty by which he agreed to share
the Levant with Egypt, so as to concentrate on the mounting Assyrian
menace. His son Tudhaliya IV, who succeeded him in 1250 BC, was to be the
last great Hittite ruler. Under his reign the capital Hattusas, which housed a
cuneiform archive, much of which has survived to the present day, was
renovated on a grand scale. The monumental work of this period, such as the
gates and the citadel, or the rock sanctuary at Yazilikaya on the edge of the city,
show strong Syrian, and especially Hurrian, influences.
The Hittites still kept tight control over Syria from their strongholds at
Aleppo and at Carchemish on the Euphrates. At that time, Ugarit was

enjoying a period of great prosperity, thanks to its location at the junction between the great land roads of the Near East and the sea roads of the eastern Mediterranean. The nearby island of Cyprus, "the isle of copper", played a major role in the city's rise to glory. No less than eight different languages were commonly spoken there, and five different systems of writing practised. One of these, an alphabetic script derived from cuneiform, was used to transcribe the local language, and became the repository of a substantial literary heritage from which much can be learned about the mythological beliefs of the Levant.

Since the way was blocked to the west by the Hittite hegemony over Syria, an expansionist Assyria inevitably turned to the south, where Babylon was an easy target. Replying to an attack by the Kassite king Kashtiliashu IV, Tukulti-Ninurta I (1244–1208 BC), the son of Shalmaneser I, captured Babylon, which he comprehensively looted and burned. Part of the population was deported, including many scribes, who took with them a substantial number of written tablets. As a result, the principal consequence of Babylon's defeat at the hands of Assyria would prove to be the definitive assimilation of Assyria into ancient Mesopotamian culture.

As for the Kassite dynasty, it was never able fully to recover from this disaster. It was left in charge of an economically enfeebled state, whose fragility was enhanced by an administrative structure founded on the tradition of making gifts of land to leading dignitaries. These donations were recorded on stone stelae known as *kudurru* which were inscribed with the symbols of the ma-

14th-13th century BC, Ras
Shamra (formerly Ugarit),
gold,
diameter 18.8 cm (7 3/8 in).
Musée du Louvre, Paris.

MAN WITH A KID, PRAYING
12th century BC, Susa,
gold,
height 7.5 cm (3 in).
Musée du Louvre, Paris.

jor gods to ensure their protection. From this practice there emerged a class of great landowners, whose wealth threatened to fragment the power of the state. The final blow was delivered by the Elamite king, Shutruk-Nahhunte[1], who crossed the river Ulai at the head of his army in 1158 BC. The lands of Babylon were overrun once more, and its glorious cities sacked. Shutruk-Nahhunte returned to Susa with the statue of the god Marduk as well as many of the great monuments of Mesopotamian history, including the victory stele of Naram-Sin and the code of Hammurabi. There could be no more eloquent sign that Kassite power had come to an end.

The collapse of Babylon was in fact merely the latest in a series of catastrophes that had befallen many formerly great states. The most striking victim of this trend was the Hittite empire, which disappeared around 1200 BC. Undermined by an economic and political crisis, it succumbed to the vast migratory movements which were laying waste much of Anatolia. Among those who passed through the region were the "Peoples of the Sea", who would eventually travel right along the coast of the eastern Mediterranean as far as the Egyptian frontier. The fall of the Hittite empire and the withdrawal of Egypt left a political vacuum in the Levant which the small-scale kingdoms that sprang up in the wake of the "Peoples of the Sea" could only partly fill. Some of these states were the creation of incomers –

1. Founder of the Shutrukide dynasty in Elam, which supplanted the Igihalkide dynasty, whose principal ruler, Untash-Napirisha, had brought about a renaissance in Elamite power at the end of the 14th century BC, symbolised by the building of a new capital on the site of Choga Zanbil.

Phrygians in Anatolia or Philistines in Canaan – while others were the resurrection of earlier local traditions, such as the neo-Hittite kingdoms in Syria and Anatolia, or the Phoenician cities along the Mediterranean coast. It was also at more or less this time that the Hebrews moved into the land of Canaan. The Bible records their repeated conflicts with the Philistines, leading to the creation of an Israelite monarchy at the end of the 11th century BC. The city of Jerusalem which served as its capital had been founded at least as long ago as the 3rd millennium. This kingdom reached its peak under Solomon (970–931 BC), before splitting into two states, the kingdom of Israel, centred on the city of Samaria, and the kingdom of Judah, which kept Jerusalem as its capital. Meanwhile the Aramaeans, another West-Semitic people who were mentioned in the annals of Assyria as long ago as the 13th century BC, had embarked upon an expansionist programme as ambitious as that undertaken by the Amorites a thousand years before. They progressively invaded the plains of the Syrian interior and of Mesopotamia, where they posed an ever greater threat to the kingdoms of Assyria and Babylon. Tiglath-pileser I (1115–1077 BC), one of Ashur's more competent and energetic kings, was able to contain them for a while, prosecuting twenty-eight separate campaigns against them in quick suc-

cession. In the course of this struggle, he became the first Assyrian king to lead his army across the Euphrates. In Babylon, a new ruler from Isin, named Nebuchadnezzar I (1124–1103 BC), was able to restore a little of its former glory to the already ancient city. Having defeated the king of Elam on the banks of the Ulai, he entered Susa and returned in triumph with the statue of Marduk, which was once again placed in its sanctuary in Babylon. But no worthy successor was forthcoming, and after his glorious reign Babylon soon relapsed into long centuries of inexorable decline. Assyria, too, was in trouble. Trade was increasingly disrupted by the expansion of the Aramaean tribes, and the kingdom was gradually forced to retreat within the boundaries of its original heartland in the foothills of the Zagros.

The Assyrian conquest of the East (934–745 BC)

It was only at the end of the 10th century, while the Aramaeans were laying siege to Nineveh, that Assyria began to recover from this setback. Under Ashurdan II (934–912 BC), Adadnirari II (911–891 BC), and Tukulti-Ninurta II (890–884 BC), the kingdom was restored to its former economic and military power. Assyrian rulers began to take the initiative

Left
KUDURRU BEARING GULA'S IMAGE
Kassite Dynasty, Mesopotamia,
black limestone,
36 x 20 cm (14 1/8 x 7 7/8 in).
Musée du Louvre, Paris.

Gula, the goddess of medicine,
is seen here surrounded by the
symbols of the major
Mesopotamian divinities.

Right
KUDURRU BEARING GULA'S IMAGE
Detail.

STATUE OF ASHURNASIRPAL II
Assyrian empire, Nimrud
(formerly Kalhu),
limestone,
height 106 cm (41 3/4 in).
British Museum, London.

The Assyrian king is shown holding
the emblems of royal authority.

KING MAKING A RITUAL OFFERING
Assyrian empire, Nimrud
(formerly Kalhu),
glazed brick,
height 30 cm (11 3/4 in).
British Museum, London.

in their struggle with the Aramaeans, and were able to force several of their leaders to pay them tribute.

The accession to the throne of Ashurnasirpal II (883–859 BC), the son of Tukulti-Ninurta II, marked a turning point in the progress of the empire. Each year, he would lead his army on campaigns to reinforce his control over the great western trade routes. In 877 BC he went as far as the Mediterranean, where he extracted heavy tribute from the coastal cities. Ashurnasirpal prosecuted his campaigns with an extraordinary cruelty that is described without any sense of shame in the inscriptions recording these expeditions. His aim was to impose his authority over a still fragile empire by means of terror. Tribute and taxes, collected annually from the peoples whom he subjugated, made Assyria rich. This wealth found expression in a major architectural project: a new capital was built at Kalhu (known today as Nimrud), a small town to the north of Ashur, which was closer to the scene of the empire's western ambitions. The town was surrounded by a wall seven kilometres (over four miles) long. Above it rose a citadel which contained a vast palace and a temple complex. This palace was to serve as a model for all Assyrian palaces to come. It consisted of two parts, each built on an identical plan organised around a central courtyard.

THE CAMP OF THE ASSYRIAN ARMY
Assyrian empire, Nimrud
(formerly Kalhu),
gypsum,
height 90 cm (35 1/2 in).
British Museum, London.

The *babanu* was the seat of the royal administration and gave onto the city outside. The *bitanu* housed the private apartments of the king. These two parts met at the throne room, where official audiences were held amid a magnificent decor of painted and carved reliefs illustrating the prowess of the king as soldier and hunter.

Ashurnasirpal died before work on the new capital was finished, and it was his son, Shalmaneser III (858–824 BC), who oversaw the completion of the final stages. He also continued the expansionist policies of his father, taking them to a new and wholly unprecedented level. Thus in 855 BC he took control of the crossing zone on the Euphrates, where the Aramaean kingdom of Bit Adini had been established. An Assyrian governor was installed in the capital of Til Barsib, which was renamed Kar-Shalmaneser. Having secured his hold over the Euphrates, Shalmaneser III then turned his attention back to the west. His advance was blocked in 853 BC near Qarqar on the Orontes by an extensive coalition made up of the principal Levantine kingdoms under the leadership of the Aramaean king of Damascus, Hadad-Ezer. Relationships with Babylon, whose prestige had survived intact, remained friendly for the most part, and Shalmaneser even came to the help of King Marduk-zakir-shumi when he was threatened by a revolt led by his

brother. When Shalmaneser died, he left behind him a substantially larger empire than that which he had inherited. But this very extension of Assyrian territory was in itself the cause of its fragility. As a result, the power of the major governors grew, and dynastic conflicts intensified.

Shalmaneser's son, Shamshi-Adad V (823–811 BC), nevertheless managed to hang on to the territories his father left him, and even added Babylon to the empire, after a war that lasted four years. The Assyrian king now ruled over lands stretching from the Gulf to the Mediterranean, as the kings of Akkad had done one and a half thousand years earlier. But Shamshi-Adad died before his time, and his son Adadnirari III (810–783 BC) was too young to govern. For five years the queen mother Shammuramat held the reigns of power. Her memory was to inspire the Greek legend of Semiramis. Royal authority was no longer powerful enough to keep control over the whole empire, and some of the provincial governors began to behave like local rulers. Under Adadnirari III and his three sons, Assyria's star was briefly in eclipse.

The age of Assyrian hegemony (745–612 BC)

On the death of the last son of Adadnirari III, the throne was seized by a usurper by the name of Tiglath-pileser III (744–727 BC). He turned the Assyrian army into a true professional corps, and undertook the conquest of the Levant. He was opposed by a coalition of neo-Hittite kingdoms led by Sarduri II, the ruler of Urartu, a kingdom which had emerged in the high

KING ASHURBANIPAL ON HIS CHARIOT
Detail. Assyrian empire, Nineveh,
Mosul marble,
height 162 cm (63 3/4 in).
Musée du Louvre, Paris.

Above right
SARGON II RECEIVING A DIGNITARY
Assyrian empire,
Khorsabad Palace (formerly Dur
Sharrukin),
Mosul marble,
height 330 cm (130 in).
Musée du Louvre, Paris.

PROCESSION OF TRIBUTE-BEARERS

Assyrian empire, Khorsabad
(formerly Dur Sharrukin),
Mosul marble,
height 162 cm (63 3/4 in).
Musée du Louvre, Paris.

The man on the right is carrying a
scale-model of their city as a sign
of its surrender.

**ROYAL SERVANTS CARRYING THE
CHARIOT OF KING SARGON II**

Assyrian empire,
Khorsabad Palace
(formerly Dur Sharrukin),
Mosul marble,
height 286 cm (112 5/8 in).
Musée du Louvre, Paris.

**CAPTURE OF THE CITY OF LACHISH
BY THE ARMY OF SENNACHERIB**

Assyrian empire, Nineveh,
gypsum,
167.6 x 190.5 cm (66 x 75 in).
British Museum, London.

THE GARDEN PARTY RELIEF

Assyrian empire, Nineveh,
Mosul marble,
height 55 cm (21 5/8 in).
British Museum, London.

King Ashurbanipal and his wife
are shown sitting in the palace
garden, where the head of the
defeated Elamite king hangs
from a tree.

CAMP OF THE ELAMITES DEPORTED
BY ASHURBANIPAL

Assyrian empire, Nineveh,
Mosul marble,
height 41 cm (16 1/8 in).
Musée du Louvre, Paris.

**A FAMILY OF DEPORTED ELAMITES
ESCORTED BY A SOLDIER**
Detail. Assyrian empire, Nineveh,
Mosul marble,
height 162 cm (63 3/4 in).
Musée du Louvre, Paris.

DEPORTED ELAMITES
Detail. Assyrian empire, Nineveh,
Mosul marble,
height 162 cm (63 3/4 in).
Musée du Louvre, Paris.

WOUNDED LIONESS

Assyrian empire, Nineveh,
Mosul marble,
160 x 120 cm (63 x 47 1/4 in).
British Museum, London.

This image demonstrated King
Ashurbanipal's prowess as a
hunter.

mountains of eastern Anatolia in the 9th century BC. The coalition was defeated in 743 BC, and thereafter the main Syrian states fell like dominoes: Arpad, then Unqi, and finally Damascus in 732. The losers were not simply made to pay annual tribute, but were fully annexed to the Assyrian state, becoming provinces of the empire. Large sections of the population were deported in order to discourage attempts at resistance. The governors were chosen from among the *sha reshi* – eunuchs whose authority depended entirely upon the will of the king – so as to prevent the provinces turning into local power bases for families that might come to challenge the royal house. The only exception to this rule was, once again, Babylon, where in 729 Tiglath-pileser himself assumed the crown, preferring to run two monarchies in parallel rather than take the risk of annexation.

This policy was continued under his son, Shalmaneser V (726–722 BC), who also rekindled Assyria's expansionist ambitions in the west. In 723, he laid siege to Samaria, the capital of the kingdom of Israel, which finally fell after a protracted struggle lasting two years. By then, Sargon II (721–705 BC) had seized the throne of Assyria. The new king again defeated a Levantine coalition at Qarqar, before going on to take Gaza despite Egypt's attempts to protect this strategic port on the Mediterranean. He even ventured "beyond the sea", as far as Cyprus, where he received tribute from seven of the island's princes. To the north of this immense empire, which now reached as far as the borders of Egypt, two states shared dominion over

Anatolia, and posed a constant threat to Assyria: in the centre, the Phrygian king Mita (who was probably the Midas of Greek myth) ruled over a prosperous and united kingdom, while in the east Urartu had been an enemy to be reckoned with for over a century. After taking Carchemish in 717, Sargon II turned his attention to the king of Urartu, Rusa I, whom he defeated in a lightning-swift campaign in 714. A narrative of this eighth campaign has survived, in the form of a letter to the god Ashur, telling of the capture and sack of the sacred city of Musasir. Having witnessed the humiliation of his neighbour, the Phrygian king Mita decided the better part of valour was to enter into an alliance with Sargon II.

The great military leader was also a gifted administrator: he reorganised the army, reinforcing the crucial cavalry and chariot sections, and built a network of roads and staging posts to speed up transmission of the royal post throughout the empire. He also began work on a new capital named in his honour – Dur Sharrukin, "Sargon's Fortress" – on a previously empty site to the north of Nineveh. Only the citadel had been completed, standing astride the city walls, with a huge, magnificently decorated palace and a tall ziggurat, when Sargon died in 705 while on a campaign in Anatolia.

His body was never found. His son Sennacherib (704–681 BC), who interpreted this disappearance as a bad omen, decided to abandon Dur Sharrukin, leaving it forever unfinished. Instead, he established his capital at Nineveh. "The city beloved of the goddess Ishtar" was extended and surrounded by a massive wall. A significant programme of work was undertaken to supply both the city and the surrounding farmland with water. At the centre of the town, Sennacherib had built "a palace without rival", richly decorated with painted and sculpted reliefs. Assyrian art was growing ever more realistic, and was never more so than here, in the depiction of the subjugated peoples. At the same time, a royal park was laid out around the palace, filled with exotic plants.

Sennacherib was eager to hold his empire together, despite the many revolts that threatened to tear it apart. In 701 BC, he occupied the town of Lachish in Palestine, but failed to take Jerusalem, the capital of Hezekiah, king of Judah. However, his major worries lay in Babylonia, which was governed by his eldest son, the heir to the Assyrian throne. When his son was assassinated, Sennacherib's vengeance was ruthless. He laid siege to Babylon, which resisted for fifteen months before capitulating in November 689. Instead of the respect that Assyrians had traditionally shown the holy city of the south, Sennacherib embarked upon a programme of systematic destruction, even digging canals so as to flood the town and scatter the earth on which it stood across the entire empire.

The end of Sennacherib's reign was dominated by strife between his sons, which culminated in their father's assassination. His chosen successor, Esarhaddon (680–669 BC), was eventually able to impose his power over his brothers, thanks to the support of his mother, Naqia of Aramaea. But he was handicapped by serious health problems, which impeded him in his task of governing such a vast empire. He began by restoring the city of Babylon, in the hope of securing the good will of the gods. With their support, he then turned to deal with the new threats that now menaced

KING ASHURBANIPAL HUNTING LIONS
Assyrian empire, Nineveh,
Mosul marble,
165 x 114.3 cm (65 x 45 in).
British Museum, London.

Hunting, a surrogate for war, was the commonest theme in the royal iconography.

Assyria. The Cimmerians and the Scythians, who came from the northern steppes, had begun mounting raids into Anatolia, where they eventually overthrew the kingdoms of Urartu and of Phrygia. Having consolidated his northern frontier through a combination of diplomatic and military action, Esarhaddon moved into the Levant to reassert his authority over the various vassal states. But all the while, his eyes were fixed on Egypt. The conflict between the two states had lain dormant for half a century. In 671 BC, Esarhaddon organised a great expedition, presented as a mission to "liberate" Egypt from the Nubian dynasty that was then governing it. He defeated the Pharaoh Taharqo's army three times, and on 11 July of that year entered into Memphis in triumph. However, two years later, while returning to Egypt to suppress a revolt, he died at Harran, on 1st November 669 BC.

His son Ashurbanipal (668–629 BC) inherited his throne without any great difficulty, thanks in part to an oath of loyalty that the Assyrians had already sworn to him in 672 BC. In 667 he reconquered Egypt, and three years later Assyrian troops marched up the Nile as far as Thebes. At the same time, he was waging war at the other end of the empire against the Elamite king Teumman. By the time Elam had been defeated in 653, the Pharaoh Psamtek I had taken advantage of this distraction to liberate his country from the Assyrian yoke and found the Saite dynasty. By this time, the Assyrian empire had demonstrably reached the limits of its military and administrative capacities. Egypt would never be reconquered, and the following year a revolt in Babylonia sounded the death-knell of an exhausted state. Assyria was plunged into a prolonged civil war through which its power was inexorably worn down. Babylon was only subdued after a siege that lasted two years.

The last gem to be added to the Assyrian crown was Ashurbanipal's palace in Nineveh. The sculpted reliefs that decorated every wall with images of the sovereign's glory are an exceptional artistic achievement. Ashurbanipal also sought to preserve the cultural traditions of Mesopotamia by assembling a library of all the essential texts of the preceding thousand years, sending to Babylon for those that could not be found to hand. However, time was running out. The peoples of Iran represented an ever greater threat to the empire – the Cimmerians to the north, the Medes to the east. The state archives come to an abrupt halt in the year 639 BC. The end of the Assyrian state was imminent.

After Ashurbanipal's death, the empire was soon torn apart by dynastic conflicts. To the east, the Median king Cyaxares was able to unite the Medes and the Persians who had both lived for many centuries on the Iranian plateau, creating a vast state to take the place of Elam, which Ashurbanipal had destroyed. Meanwhile, in the south, Nabopolassar, the new king of the Chaldeans[1], had captured Babylon in 616. The two kings then independently attacked Assyria. In 614, Ashur fell to the Medes. Cyaxares and Nabopolassar met in the former capital to seal their new alliance, and then went on jointly to lay siege to Nineveh. The city which once made the world shake with fear capitulated in only three months. The Assyrian empire was over for good, and the victors divided up the spoils: Mesopotamia was annexed by Nabopolassar and Elam by Cyaxares, while Egypt recovered control of Palestine and Syria.

The Babylonian empire (612–539 BC)

After the destruction of Assyria, the Chaldean ruler of Babylon began to think of himself as the rightful successor to the enormous empire he had helped bring down. Towards the end of his life, he sent his son, the future Nebuchadnezzar II, to take the rich lands of the Levant back from the Egyptians. During the year 605 BC, the young man captured the city of Carchemish, which gave him control over navigation on the Euphrates, and went on to defeat the Egyptian army near Hama. By September, he was back in Babylon to be crowned king, following his father's death. Nebuchadnezzar II ruled over an empire that was substantially larger than those of previous Babylonian dynasties. But his control of his lands was far from secure, especially in the Levant, where the population, encouraged by Egypt, frequently revolted against their new masters. When Jerusalem refused to pay its annual tribute in 597, Nebuchadnezzar occupied the city by force. The same scenario was repeated in 587, each time accompanied by the deportation of thousands of Jews, together with their king, to

1. The Kaldu, or Chaldeans, were a people of uncertain origin who had settled in southern Babylonia at the beginning of the 1st millennium BC.

THE ESAGIL TABLET
Seleucid period,
3rd-century-BC copy
of a 6th-century-BC document,
clay,
height 18 cm (7 in).
Musée du Louvre, Paris.

This text details the dimensions of the great Esagil temple at Babylon and of the famous Tower of Babel.

Babylon. The holy city was sacked, "the house of Yahweh was burned, as was the house of the king, and all the important houses".

During the reign of Nebuchadnezzar II, Babylon was at the height of its splendour. Occupying both banks of the Euphrates, the city was enlarged and restored. It was surrounded by a double wall, punctuated by tall towers and eight monumental gates, each of which was under the protection of a particular divinity, save for the King's Gate. Beside the Ishtar Gate, decorated in glazed brick, stood the immense royal palace, which was separated from the rest of the town by its own wall. The Processional Way led along the east wall of the palace compound from the Ishtar Gate to the temple of Bel-Marduk, known as *Esagil*, "the house with the high roof". This was the route taken by the statue of Marduk during the *Akitu* festival to mark the Babylonian New Year. The Esagila complex was dominated by the great seven-storey ziggurat *Etemenanki*, "the house that is the foundation of heaven and earth". This was the building that figures in the Bible as the Tower of Babel.

After the death of Nebuchadnezzar II in 562 BC, the Babylonian empire saw its prestige and power rapidly decline. It had three new rulers in the space of six years, at a time when its allies, the Medes, were constantly adding new territories to their kingdom, having conquered Urartu and

BULL

Babylonian empire, Babylon,
Ishtar Gate,
glazed bricks.
Archaeological Museum, Istanbul.

HORNED DRAGON

Babylonian empire, Babylon,
Ishtar Gate,
glazed bricks.
Archaeological Museum, Istanbul.

The horned dragon and the bull
were the attributes of the great
Babylonian divinities, Marduk and
Ishtar.

Cappadocia in particular. The accession to the throne of Nabonidos in 556 did not help matters either. This eccentric ruler insisted on trying to impose the god Sin, to whom his mother was high priestess, as the chief god in the pantheon, thus ousting Marduk. When his attempts were roundly rejected by most of the Babylonian aristocracy, he left to spend ten years in self-imposed exile at the oasis of Tayma' in northern Arabia, leaving his son Belshazzar to govern in his place.

Meanwhile, a new power was emerging in the east, in the former lands of Elam now occupied by the Persians. Ruled by the Achaemenid dynasty – named after Achaemenes, who had founded the house in the early 7th century BC – the new country of Persis was finally unified under Cyrus II, who was crowned its king in 559 BC. His accession marked the beginning of an astonishing period of expansion. In 550, he defeated his overlord, the Median king Astyages, thus extending his power at a single blow far into the heart of Anatolia. Three years later, the rest of Anatolia came under his jurisdiction when he defeated Croesus, king of the wealthy kingdom of Lydia, at Pteria. Cyrus then turned to the east, where he gradually imposed his rule over the whole of the Iranian plateau, and as far as central Asia. In each of the countries that he conquered, he was careful to support the local aristocracy and respect local traditions. His policy was so effective, that when he decided to attack Babylon, he found many Babylonians happy to embrace him and get rid of Nabonidos. The Babylonian army, which was much smaller than the Persian forces, was defeated on the banks of the Tigris, and Cyrus was able to enter the ancient city without resistance on 23 October 539 BC.

The Persian empire (539–330 BC)

By annexing Babylon and its empire, the Achaemenid dynasty inherited the cultural legacy of Mesopotamia in particular, and the Near East in general. Cambyses II, who succeeded his father Cyrus II in 530 BC, went on to conquer Egypt, adding both its lands and its culture to the Persian domain. The result was an empire whose universal ambitions were reminiscent of those of Sargon of Akkad two thousand years earlier, but which was pursuing its plan on a scale never previously seen in the region. If Babylon was still an important religious and cultural centre, political power henceforth resided in Iran, at the heart of Persis (modern Fars), where Cyrus founded his capital, Pasargadae.

On the death of Cambyses in 522 BC, a violent civil war broke out between different branches of the Achaemenid dynasty. Darius I (522–486 BC) emerged victorious from this struggle, and after suppressing numerous revolts across his empire, was able to push its eastern frontier back as far as the Indus. So as to reinforce the unity of this gigantic state, he undertook a systematic reorganisation of its administration. He divided the empire into provinces, each of which was governed by a satrap, chosen from among those close to the Great King. Darius built his own capital on the site of Persepolis, forty kilometres (25 miles) south of Cyrus' city. The main administration of the empire was located somewhat more centrally in the

CAPITAL WITH BULLS

Achaemenid empire,
Susa,
limestone,
height 552 cm (18 ft).
Musée du Louvre, Paris.

This capital comes from one of the thirty-six columns, each 20 m (65 ft) high, of the great hypostyle hall in the palace of Darius I at Susa.

TWO WINGED LIONS WITH HUMAN HEADS

Achaemenid empire,
Susa,
glazed bricks,
120 x 117 cm (47 1/4 x 46 in).
Musée du Louvre, Paris.

AN AUDIENCE WITH XERXES I

Achaemenid empire,
Persepolis, relief from the
Treasury.

Tehran Museum, Iran.

ancient city of Susa. Craftsmen and materials were brought from every province of the empire to build the vast palaces of Susa and Persepolis with their magnificent hypostyle halls. The result was a syncretic art, mixing Mesopotamian, Egyptian and Greek influences.

The defeat of the Persians in the Graeco-Persian Wars marked the limits of the empire's expansion. After the reign of Xerxes I (486–465 BC), the monarchy was increasingly preoccupied with intrigues at court, rather than the pursuit of strategic power. The result was a slow decline, which culminated in humiliation at the hands of Alexander of Macedon. Having defeated the armies of Darius III three times between 334 and 331 BC, Alexander was able to take over the reins of the vast empire and assume the succession of the Achaemenid dynasty. He died in Babylon in 323 BC. His death marked the end of an era. Greek hegemony would soon be followed by that of Rome, which in turn would give way to a new world unified by the religion of Islam – a world that is in many ways the heir to the age-long traditions of the ancient Near East.

4. Writing and knowledge

Pages 144–145
PICTOGRAPHIC TABLETS
Late 4th millennium BC,
southern Mesopotamia,
clay,
5.2 x 7.8 cm (2 x 3 in).
Musée du Louvre, Paris.

A human head beside a bowl
and an ear of wheat refers to
the ration of cereals given as
payment for a particular task.

The first known written documents date from circa 3300 BC. They were found in southern Mesopotamia, at the site of what was then in the process of becoming the city of Uruk. The invention of writing comes right at the end of the long process of cultural evolution that led from the Neolithic age to the birth of the city and, with it, a differentiated, hierarchical society. Writing began as a coherent system of pictographic signs, in which each image represented an object or an idea. But as early as 3000 BC it began to shift from representing things to representing sounds. The invention of phonetic script "was facilitated by changes made to the signs themselves, which were decomposed into a series of smaller elements, shaped like nails or wedges – whence the name, cuneiform. This new script allowed the complete transcription of language with not only its vocabulary but also its grammatical structure. Yet it remained a hybrid system, in which each cuneiform sign had both phonetic and ideographic values.

**TABLET WITH ARCHAIC
CUNEIFORM TEXT**
Archaic Sumerian
Dynasties,
Telloh (formerly Girsu),
clay,
7.8 x 7.8 cm (3 x 3 in).
Musée du Louvre, Paris.

Tally of sheep and goats,
found in a temple.

**PLAQUE IN THE FORM OF A
BEARD WITH CUNEIFORM TEXT**
Archaic Sumerian
Dynasties, Umma,
gold,
*8.5 x 6.7 cm
(3 3/8 x 2 5/8 in).*
Musée du Louvre, Paris.

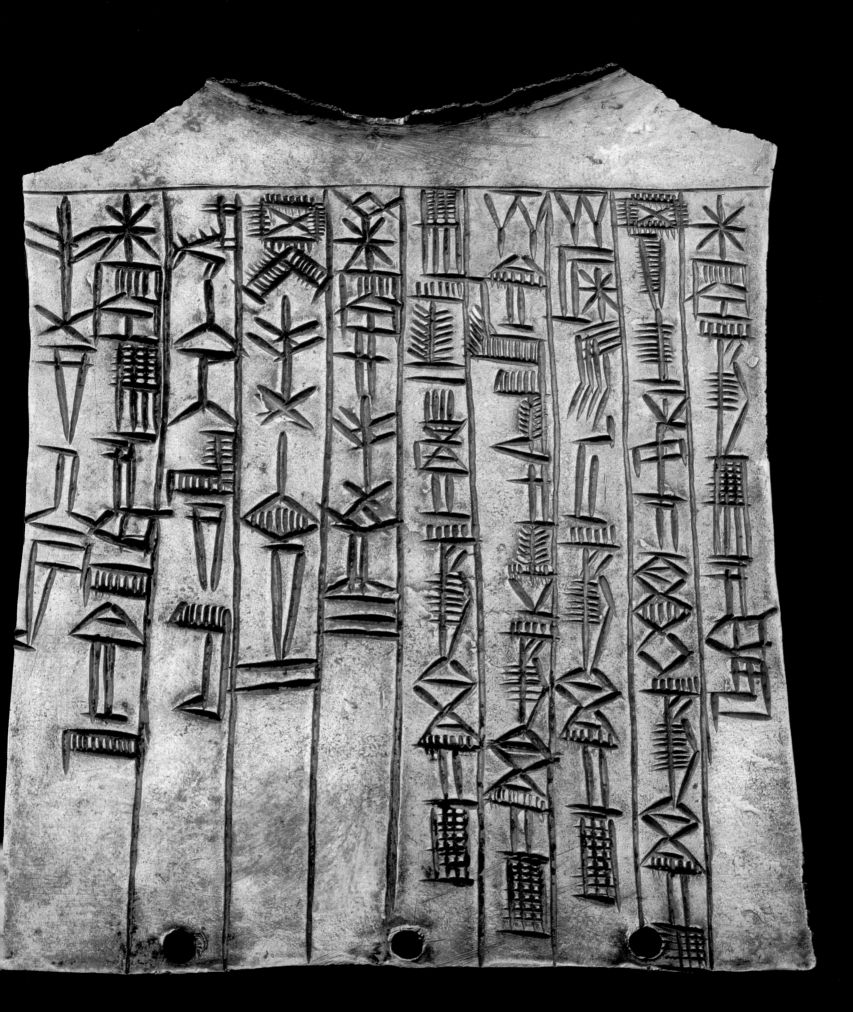

The evolution of writing

The first language to be transcribed was Sumerian, which was probably the language spoken by the people who invented writing. Then came Akkadian, followed by the two dialects that derived from it, Babylonian and Assyrian. At the same time, the cuneiform system was being adopted by the other major languages of the Near East, such as Elamite, Eblaite, Hurrian and Hittite. Akkadian cuneiform rapidly established itself as the principal vehicle of diplomatic relations and trade. In the 2nd millennium, a new simplified form of writing appeared. It was based on alphabets with a limited number of signs, each corresponding to a basic phonetic unit. The alphabet was invented in the Levant, where Egyptian hieroglyphs and Mesopotamian cuneiform met. Its different forms are sometimes closer to hieroglyphs (e.g. the Sinai alphabet), sometimes to cuneiform (e.g. the Ugaritic alphabets). By the end of the 2nd millennium, however, there was only one alphabet in use: the linear consonantal Phoenician alphabet. This in turn came to serve as the origin of the main later alphabets of the region: Hebrew, Aramaic, and even Greek. In the course of the 1st millennium, these alphabets would begin to rival cuneiform writing throughout the newly-unified Near East, especially Aramaic, which was at different times the official language of the Assyrian, Babylonian and Persian empires. After the victory of Alexander the Great, Greek became the principle vehicle of the Hellenisation of the Near East. Cuneiform was henceforth used only for recording religious and scientific knowledge, yet even in this restricted function it survived in southern Mesopotamia until the 2nd century AD.

The transmission of knowledge

Over the first three millennia of its existence, the art of writing was essentially transmitted from one generation to another by scribes. It was an instrument of both power and knowledge, and as such initiation was confined to a small elite. "Of all the human trades that exist on earth and of which the god Enlil has named the names, none is more difficult than the art of the scribe", one scribe confided to his son who was intending to follow in his footsteps. It was a difficult art, but also a most prestigious one. It required a long and rigorous period of training, of which the greater part was spent in the house of a master, known in Sumerian as an *edubba*, or "tablet-house". Depending on how much knowledge he had acquired, and on his social origins, a young scribe might then become a "public scrivener", a temple administrator, or a member of the corps of the royal palace. These great institutions gradually came to employ an ever greater number of scribes, assigned to ever more specific functions. They also began to assemble archives and libraries, repositories of their society's collective memory, storehouses – and workshops – for information and knowledge.

Certain of the more erudite scribes devoted themselves entirely to the preservation and nurturing of human knowledge, even though in the ancient Near East knowledge was never independent of some more prag-

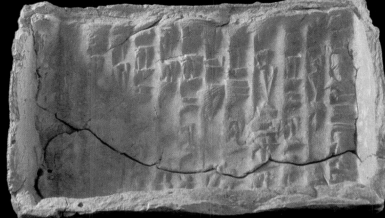

**INSCRIPTION IN PHOENICIAN
ALPHABETIC SCRIPT**

Detail. 5th century BC, Sidon,
basalt,
*119 x 256 cm
(46 7/8 x 100 3/4 in).*
Musée du Louvre, Paris.

Above
**INSCRIPTION IN ARAMAEAN
ALPHABETIC SCRIPT**

Detail. 7th century BC,
Neirab,
basalt,
93 x 34 cm (36 5/8 x 13 3/8 in).
Musée du Louvre, Paris.

**TABLET WITH CUNEIFORM TEXT AND
ENVELOPE**

Third Dynasty of Ur,
Mesopotamia,
clay,
4.3 x 6.7 cm (1 3/4 x 2 5/8 in).
Musée du Louvre, Paris.

This financial document was
obviously a private communication,
and was therefore carried in a
sealed envelope.

CUNEIFORM ALPHABET

14th century BC, Ras Shamra
(formerly Ugarit),
clay,
5.5 x 6 cm (2 1/8 x 2 3/8 in).
Musée du Louvre, Paris.

This fragment of a tablet lists the
characters of a cuneiform alphabet used in the city of Ugarit to
transcribe the local language.

matic aim. The role of these men of letters, who were known as *ummanu*,
was to identify, transcribe and interpret the messages they received from
the world. Just as thought is expressed in writing, so the universe can be
deciphered through the signs that nature presents to man. These signs contain glimpses of the fate of men and nations. They are very diverse: found
above all in the major vehicles of divination – the entrails of animals and
the movement of the stars – they are also present in unusual objects and
unexpected events. As such, they were faithfully recorded, together with
their supposed consequences, in the form of lists of omens. These lists were
then regularly copied out and added to, until eventually the major series of
the different kinds of omen had been defined.

By the accumulation of observations, the scribes arrived at a casuistical system not only for interpreting signs, but also for solving problems. The
cases collected were classified into appropriate categories, and theories
could then be elaborated by analogy to cover circumstances which had not
yet arisen. This led to the composition of veritable treatises covering the
principal branches of speculative thought – whether mathematics,
medicine or jurisprudence. Thus the so-called legal "codes" were in fact
anthologies of cases accompanied by the sentences that had been pro-

nounced on them. These treatises were an extension of the taste for systematic classification that was expressed earlier in the great lexical lists that accompanied the invention of writing. They are part of the same attempt to introduce some sort of logical order into the universe.

In this way, real knowledge concerning recognisably scientific fields of study began to develop. Mathematics is a case in point. The need to keep reliable accounts led to the elaboration of two different numerical systems. The most widely-used was sexagesimal, the other decimal. Tables were also devised to assist with calculations (multiplication, square and cubic roots, and inverse ratios). By the end of the 3rd millennium, a positional system of numbers had been introduced, using an empty space to signify an absent unit until the zero was invented at the end of the 1st millennium. Another important class of documents was devoted to the exposition of mathematical problems and their solutions, either individually or grouped together by themes. From these texts, it is clear that second-degree equations, the calculation of surfaces and volumes, and even Pythagoras' theorem, were all familiar to the Mesopotamians.

In the field of astronomy, as well as a calendar based on the lunar year, there are texts which record repeated observations of the night sky, giving particular weight to eclipses of the sun, moon and various planets, with a view to extracting astrological information from these raw data. Two categories of stars were distinguished: on the one hand, the fixed stars, which are arranged in constellations "attached" to the heavenly vault and move with it; and on the other, the wandering stars, such as the Moon, the Sun, the five known planets, comets and shooting stars. Sixty-six constellations and individual stars are listed in the important anthology of heavenly omens known as the *mul apin*. There they are divided into three celestial

"ways", associated with the three great gods, Anu, Enlil and Ea, and surrounded by the eighteen constellations of the zodiac which follow the annual path of the Sun. It was only in the 5th century BC that the number of zodiac signs was reduced to the twelve we are familiar with today, so as to correspond to the twelve months of the year. The steady accumulation of observations led the Mesopotamians to recognise the recurrent nature of certain phenomena in the night sky, and this enabled them to predict their return. Slowly but surely, genuine astronomical knowledge was being built up, and methods of calculation were developed which allowed the mechanics of the planets and stars to be described with some accuracy, as is shown by the models used to calculate astronomical tables and almanacs.

If Mesopotamian astronomy was a genuine science, Mesopotamian medicine remained an essentially empirical matter of hit-and-miss, surrounded by a heavily magical aura. A doctor *(asu)* often worked in tandem with an exorcist *(ashippu)*, whose role was to expel those illnesses that were inflicted as a punishment for sin, or by chance moral contagion. The *asu* for his part would rely on an anthology of past diagnoses, based on the description of symptoms, whether local or general. The diagnosis would be accompanied by a prognosis on the likely evolution of the illness, and

advice on recommended therapeutic action. Some of the proposed treatments were magical in character, while others used remedies based on natural products, whether animal, mineral or (above all) vegetable. This empirical pharmacopoeia was presented in the form of a list of ingredients, together with instructions for their preparation and administration.

Mesopotamian knowledge always remained essentially empirical in nature. The aim was to find practical solutions to practical problems, and so long as the solution approximated what was required, no energy was expended on unnecessary theorising. Observations were accumulated, but never seem to have led to the postulation of general laws. Yet the writing of classificatory lists and casuistical treatises is evidence of a determination to order the world. Logical thought found expression in a unified conception of the universe, in which all its elements are interrelated through a vast network of symbolic correspondences. The organising principles of this network are analogy and dialectical opposition. The world it defines is a dynamic world, which remains intelligible despite its infinite diversity. Nature is not a collection of brute facts, but a realm of signs, and the stage of myth.

MATHEMATICAL TABLET

Circa 1800 BC, Sippar,
clay,
33.5 x 28 cm (13 1/8 x 11 in).
British Museum, London.

The text and diagrams deal with a number of geometrical problems in architecture.

Pages 162–163
LUCKY PLAQUE TO WARD OFF THE DEMON LAMASHTU
Assyrian empire, Mesopotamia,
bronze,
13.8 x 8.8 cm (5 1/2 x 3 1/2 in).
Musée du Louvre, Paris.

Beneath the symbols of the gods and the procession of the seven demons is a scene representing an exorcism ceremony. While the sick man languishes in bed, Lamashtu is pressed to return into hell. She is shown leaving, seated on her donkey in her boat. On the reverse side is an image of her husband Pazuzu, who is invoked to come to the sick man's aid.

course, but also sacred hymns and even scientific treatises and anthologies of wise sayings. Through these many fragments, certain recurrent elements stand out, which suggest a common perspective, if not a single story. From these we can deduce that in Mesopotamia the origins of the world were never conceived of as a creation, in the sense of the act of a creator-god, but rather as a natural process, whose internal evolution led to the visible order of the cosmos and from which the different gods and goddesses themselves emerged.

The original state of the universe was a state of indifferentiation. It consisted of a single element: the primordial waters, the great cosmic fluid from which all things come. This cosmic water later took on the form of a goddess. The Sumerians called her Nammu, who was both the primordial Sea and "the Mother who gave birth to heaven and earth" *(Ama.Tu.An.Ki)*. The Sumerian myth of *Enki and Ninmah* defines her as "Nammu, the initial mother, who gave birth to the numberless gods".

During the Babylonian period, the *Enuma elish* (the Akkadian name for the myth also known as "The Epic of Creation") presents a similar conception of the primordial universe as a state of indifferentiation. In this later work, the first state of the world consists in the union of two liquid substances that were later separated: Tiamat, the salt waters of the sea, and Apsu, the great freshwater ocean.

> *"When skies above were not yet named*
> *Nor earth below pronounced by name,*
> *Apsu, the first one, their begetter*
> *And maker Mummu Tiamat, who bore them all,*
> *Had mixed their waters together."*
> (*Enuma elish*, lines 1–5.)

Yet this cosmic fluid which contained the entire universe was destined to be rent apart, so that difference could emerge in the midst of indifferentiation. This first act of separation, which founded the organised universe, divided the heavens *(An)* from the earth *(Ki)*, the Above from the Below. This event is described in several texts, including the Sumerian myth of *Gilgamesh, Enkidu and Hell:*

> *"That day, that far-off day,*
> *That night, that far-off night…*
> *That former day when what was necessary appeared*
> *That former day when what was necessary was made*
> *with care, as was fitting…*
> *When the sky distanced itself from the earth,*
> *When the god An had carried off the sky,*
> *When the god Enlil had carried off the earth,*
> *And had given hell as a dowry to the goddess Ereshkigal…"*

There was thus a mythical day on which the original separation took place, and the world was born. "That day, that far-off day" represents a sort

HEAD OF A GOD
Late 3rd millennium BC,
Telloh (formerly Girsu),
clay,
10.8 x 6.4 cm (4 1/4 x 2 1/2 in).
Musée du Louvre, Paris

The cap with its four pairs of horns is an emblem of divine status.

HEAD OF A GOD.
Detail.

of horizon for all cosmological speculation, the first day on which there was a cosmos distinct from the preceding chaos. The separation of earth and sky is both an act in time, and the act by which time comes into being. The universe then begins to acquire a structure. It is generally conceived of as a spherical space, organised into three superposed levels.

– The sky (*An* in Sumerian, *sham* in Akkadian) is the upper level, the Above, which can be further subdivided into several celestial levels. It is usually thought of as a liquid mass held in place by the heavenly vault. In this vault are fixed the lights which illuminate the world.

– The earth (*Ki* in Sumerian, *ersetu* in Akkadian) occupies the centre of the cosmic sphere. It is a solid platform, sometimes round and sometimes square, surrounded by the salt waters of the sea and floating on the *Apsu*, the abyss of fresh water which emerges from springs to form streams and rivers across its surface.

– An underworld (*Kur* and *engur*) which forms the Below, a dark mirror-image of the heavenly Above. This is hell, the "Land-of-no-return", where the dead go when they leave the "land of the living".

There are two mobile elements which move between the fixed elements of this cosmic framework, binding them together and imparting movement to them. These are air and water, the double source of fertility and life. Like the three levels of the world, these two fluids are each associated with a god: Enlil (air) and Enki (water). The great gods appeared at the same time as the structure of the physical world, with which they are, in a sense, consubstantial. Thus the term *An* in Sumerian referred to both the sky and the god of the sky, illustrating this primordial connection between the natural elements and the gods.

The major gods and the ordering of the universe

From this moment on, the world is organised around the dynamic interplay of the gods, each of whom is responsible for a different aspect of nature. Physical structures and natural phenomena are only made possible for the Mesopotamian mind by the divine powers that inhabit them. It is the gods who set the mechanism of the cosmos in motion, and who bring forth life. Each of the gods on whom the ordering of the universe depends is endowed with his or her own personality, as well as with symbolic attributes appropriate to the role they play. Through this anthropomorphic vision, the divine realm comes to act as a sublimated projection of human life, with the distinction that the gods are supposed to possess immortality. A social drama based on the life of human communities is thus superimposed onto the allegory of nature. Gods and goddesses form couples, and are interrelated as the members of various extended families. Taking on human form, they live in palaces that are also temples, in the company of their wives and children, their courtiers and their servants. They thus serve to legitimise the power of human kings, who are confirmed in their role as privileged mediators between humanity and its gods.

The different generations of the gods provide a scale by which to measure mythical time, as well as suggesting the existence of causal relationships.

GODDESS
Second Dynasty of Lagash,
Telloh (formerly Girsu),
limestone,
16.2 x 20 cm
(6 3/8 x 7 7/8 in).
Musée du Louvre, Paris.

GODDESS
Detail.

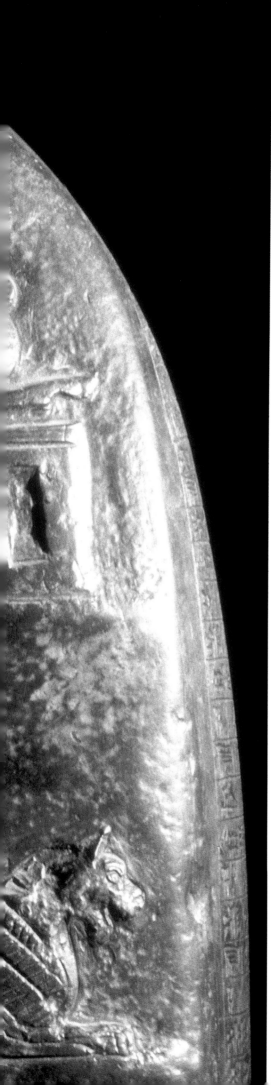

Two groups emerge: first, the "cosmic" divinities, the earliest to have appeared, who govern the basic physical structures of the world. They in turn gave birth to the "astral" divinities, who determine the course of each man's life and death.

> *"When Anu, Enlil and Ea, the great gods,*
> *Had established in their council the plans of heaven and earth,*
> *And when they had charged the great gods of the stars*
> *To produce the days and guarantee the regular succession of the months,*
> *So as to offer them to the human science of astrology,*
> *Then the sun was seen to rise,*
> *And the stars shone for ever in the sky."*
> (Prologue to the great astrological treatise *Enuma Anu Enlil*.)

The cosmic divinities
An (Anu)[1]

An was the god of the sky, where he was seen as a veritable king, the "father of the gods". He later abandoned his powers to his son Enlil, and thereafter only intervened to act as a final court of appeal or to preside over the assembly of the gods. No surviving representation of the god An has been identified for certain, nor is he clearly associated with any particular symbolic attribute, with the exception of the horned cap. This sign of divine kingship is a distant allusion to the primitive symbolism of the bull. However, there may be a confusion here with one of the attributes of Enlil. Although one of the major gods of the pantheon, An does not have a very well defined personality, since he is the very type of the divine, and as such cannot be represented.

Enlil

In Sumerian, his name means "Lord Wind". Enlil was the power that governed the movement of the air, the fluid that filled the space between the sky and the earth. As such, he also controlled life, figured metaphorically as air, wind or breath. He is thus the "between-sky-and-earth", the bond and the mediator between the levels of the world, an idea that is also expressed in another of his names, "Great Mountain". Son of An the sky and Ki the earth, Enlil became ruler over the world. It is he who possesses the "Tablet of Destiny" by which he is able to determine men's fate, as the evil bird in the myth of Anzu discovers when he spies on the god in his palace: "His eyes contemplate the attributes of the power of Enlil: his majestic crown, his divine robe, the Tablet of Destiny in his hands."

1. The name of the god in Sumerian is followed in brackets by the Akkadian name, where this differs from the former.

THE KUDURRU OF MELI-SHIPAK II
Detail. Kassite Dynasty, Susa, limestone,
65 x 30 cm (25 5/8 x 11 3/4 in).
Musée du Louvre, Paris.

At the top of this stele are the emblems of the four principal gods in the Mesopotamian pantheon: An, Enlil, Enki and Ninhursag. Above them are the symbols of the sky-gods: the crescent moon of Sin, the star of Ishtar and the solar disc of Shamash.

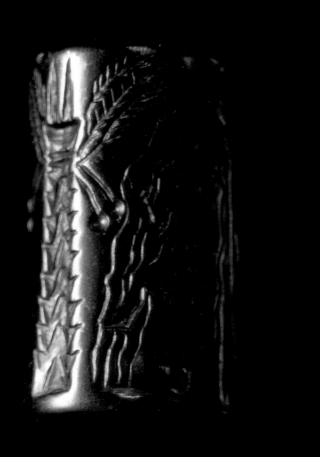

CYLINDER-SEAL AND IMPRESSION

Akkadian Dynasty,
Mesopotamia,
marble,
height 3.6 cm (1 3/8 in).
Musée du Louvre, Paris.

The theme of the seal is the
rebirth of nature in the spring,
thanks to the joint action of
the god of fresh water, Enki,
the sun-god, Shamash and
the goddess Ishtar.

His Sumerian name means "Lord Earth". He is the master of Apsu (in Sumerian Abzu), the subterranean reservoir that feeds the earth with fresh water via springs and wells. This is why he is traditionally represented with two streams of water flowing from his shoulders or from a vase that he holds in his hands. These two streams may be meant to represent the Tigris and the Euphrates. Sometimes he is depicted inside a shrine of water. His animal is the hybrid goat-fish, the mythical ancestor of the Roman Capricorn. Held to be the son of An, Enki is "he whose words are just", the master of all wisdom, whether intellectual or artistic. He is also the protector of mankind, whom he will later save from the flood.

CYLINDER-SEAL AND IMPRESSION
Akkadian Dynasty,
Mesopotamia,
marble,
height 3.6 cm (1 3/8 in).
Musée du Louvre, Paris.

This scene shows two figures being presented to the water-god Enki (Ea) by his two-faced intendant Usmu.

Ninhursag

"The Lady of the mountain" (Nin-hursag) is the very type of earthly power. She is the mountain-world that represents the earth. She is also the mother-goddess, known as Nintu, "the Lady of begetting", or as Ninmah, "the exalted Lady". The myth *Lugal-e* tells how the name Ninhursag was given to Ninmah by her son, the god Ninurta, after his victory over Asag. This demon, who was master of the Land of Stones, was defeated in single combat by Ninurta. The god piled up the stones, which were a precious commodity in the land of Sumer, into a gigantic mountain, which he placed under the protection of Ninhursag.

The astral divinities
Nanna (Sin)

The moon-god, son of Enlil and of his wife Ninlil, is the master of the months and seasons. The Mesopotamian calendar was based on lunar cycles, and the perfect regularity of the calendar was essential for the prosperity of an agrarian society. Thus one myth tells at some length how Sin came to do homage to his father, from whom he received in return guarantees of prosperity and "long life".

PERFORATED WALL PLAQUE SHOWING A LIBATION OFFERED TO THE GODDESS NINHURSAG

Detail. Archaic Sumerian Dynasties,
Telloh (formerly Girsu),
limestone,
17.4 x 16 cm (6 7/8 x 6 1/4 in).
Musée du Louvre, Paris.

RELIEF WITH THE MOON-GOD SIN

8th century BC, Harran,
limestone.
Aleppo Museum, Syria.

There was an important temple to the god Sin at Harran, symbolised here by the two staffs surmounted by a crescent moon.

The alliance of water and sunlight
is the source of all fertility. Here, it
makes the date palm grow.

Utu (Shamash)

Shamash is the sun-god, "the Lord of the torch of the totality", whose light returns every day to chase away the darkness and light up the world. As the moon governs the months, so the sun creates the days. Every morning, he emerges from the doors of the sky to the east, to spend all day travelling across the heavenly vault, until at evening he disappears again into the doors of the sky to the west. Dispensing light and warmth, he is also the source of justice among men. In his human form, he is shown with the rays of the sun shining forth from his shoulders, but he is more commonly represented by the solar disc.

Ninurta

Ninurta is, in the first place, the god of vegetation, provider of fertility and protector of agriculture. He is master of storm and rain, "the Lord of fertile ground". But in mythical narratives he appears most often in the guise of a warrior god. Besides his victory over Asag, he is the only god in the myth of Anzu who dares to confront the fabulous bird who has made off with Enlil's "Tablet of Destiny". After defeating him and restoring order to a world threatened with chaos, Ninurta takes the bird as his emblem, under the name of Imdugud, the lion-headed eagle, the thunder-bird and bringer of the storm cloud.

LION-HEADED EAGLE

Detail. Mid-3rd millennium,
Mari,
lapis lazuli and gold,
height 12.8 cm (5 in).
Damascus Museum, Syria.

The god Ninurta defeated the
storm-bird and turned him into an
emblem of his own power.

THE GODDESS ISHTAR, NAKED
Detail. Amorite Dynasties,
Larsa,
clay vase,
height 26.2 cm (10 1/4 in).
Musée du Louvre, Paris.

**THE GODDESS ISHTAR, WINGED AND
NAKED, STANDING ON TWO GOATS**
Amorite Dynasties, Larsa,
clay,
height 20.5 cm (8 in).
Musée du Louvre, Paris.

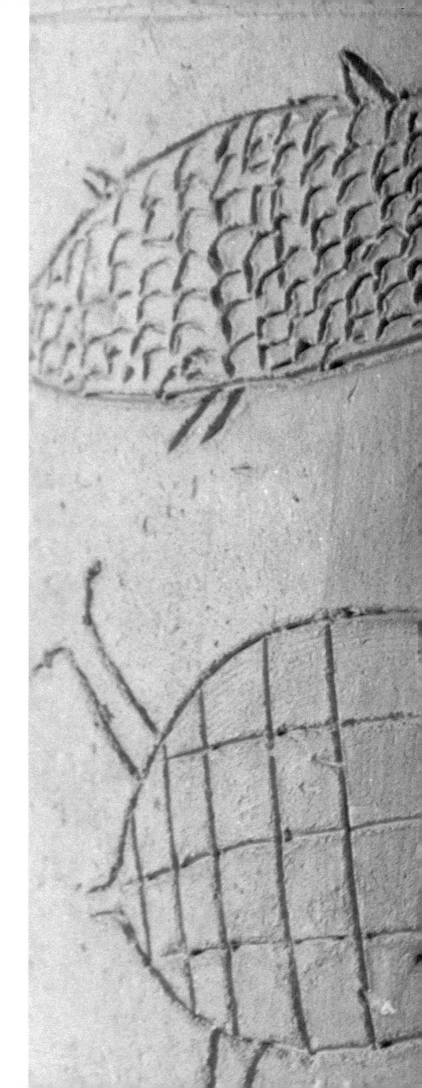

CYLINDER-SEAL AND IMPRESSION REPRESENTING THE SACRED HERD OF INANNA

Late 4th millennium BC,
Mesopotamia,
height 5.2 cm (2 in).
Musée du Louvre, Paris.

The stable with a staff planted on its roof refers symbolically to the first temples dedicated to the goddess.

Inanna (Ishtar)

Her name is a contraction of Nin-anna, which means "Lady of Heaven" in Sumerian. Initially she was a fertility goddess, the mistress of store-houses and stables. The earliest depictions of her sacred enclosure, often represented by the single staff that stood at its entrance, date from the proto-urban period at Uruk. Later, a star replaced the staff as Inanna's symbol — an allusion to Venus, the evening (and morning) star. Inanna/Ishtar was probably also the goddess of the storm, and she soon developed a war-like character, which made her one of the most fearful of the gods. In her human form, she is often shown armed and winged, standing in a triumphant attitude. Source of natural fertility, she is the mistress of human fecundity, goddess of love and sexuality. She contains within herself the inseparable powers of life and death. This is the meaning of the symbol of the lion, which is her animal attribute. The myth *The Descent of Inanna to the Underworld* (known in its Akkadian version as *The Descent of Ishtar to the Underworld*) also deals with this theme. It recounts how the goddess travels through the subterranean realm over which her sister Ereshkigal reigns. During her journey, she is forced to shed her finery in seven ritual stages. She is then held prisoner until her lover, the shepherd Dumuzi, comes and takes her place. It is through the voluntary self-sacrifice of a man that the regular cycle of natural fertility is restored to mankind.

THE ELEVENTH TABLET OF THE EPIC OF GILGAMESH

Assyrian Empire, Nineveh,
clay,
height 13.7 cm (5 3/8 in).
British Museum, London.

The narrative of the Flood figures at the beginning of this tablet.

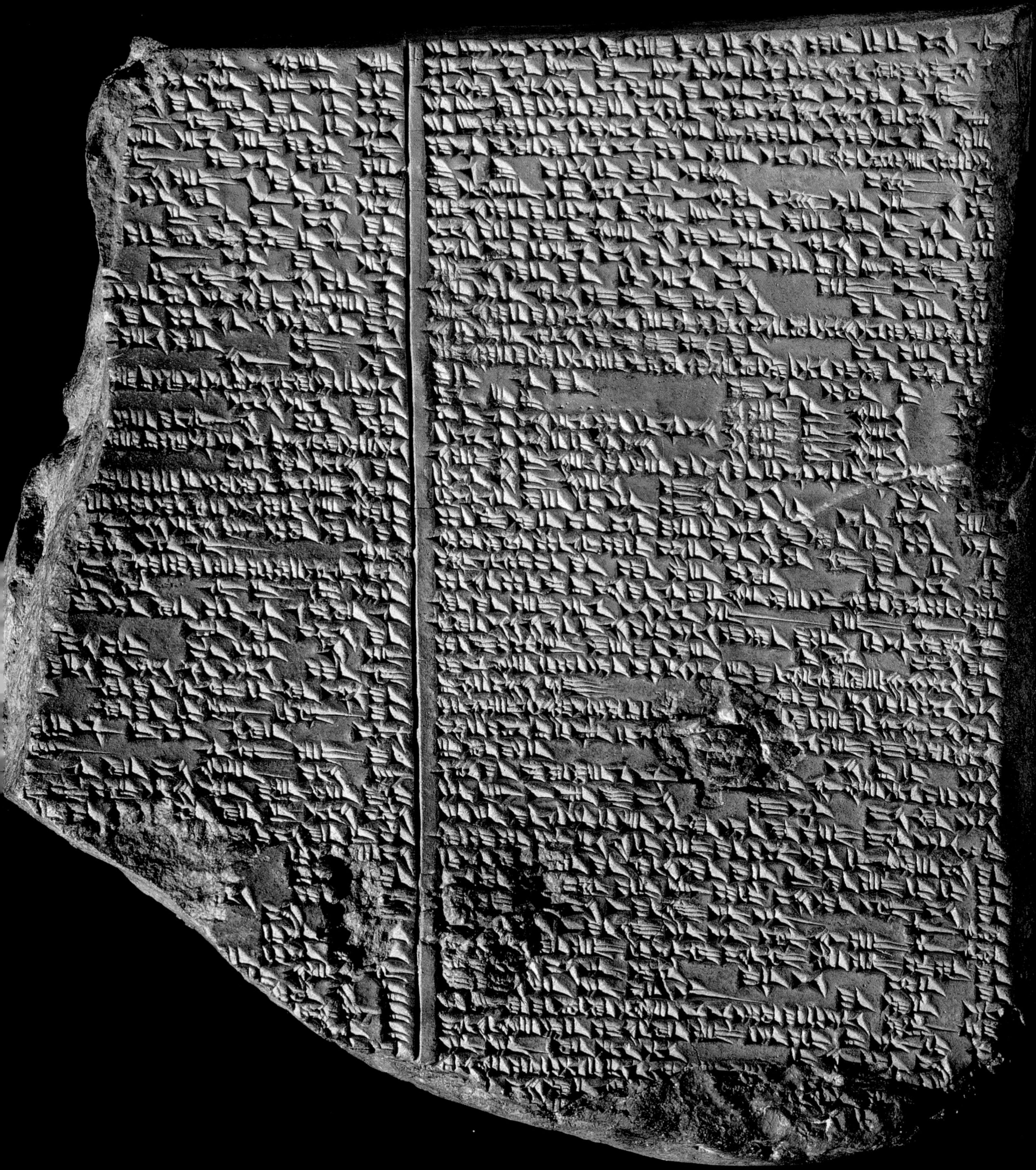

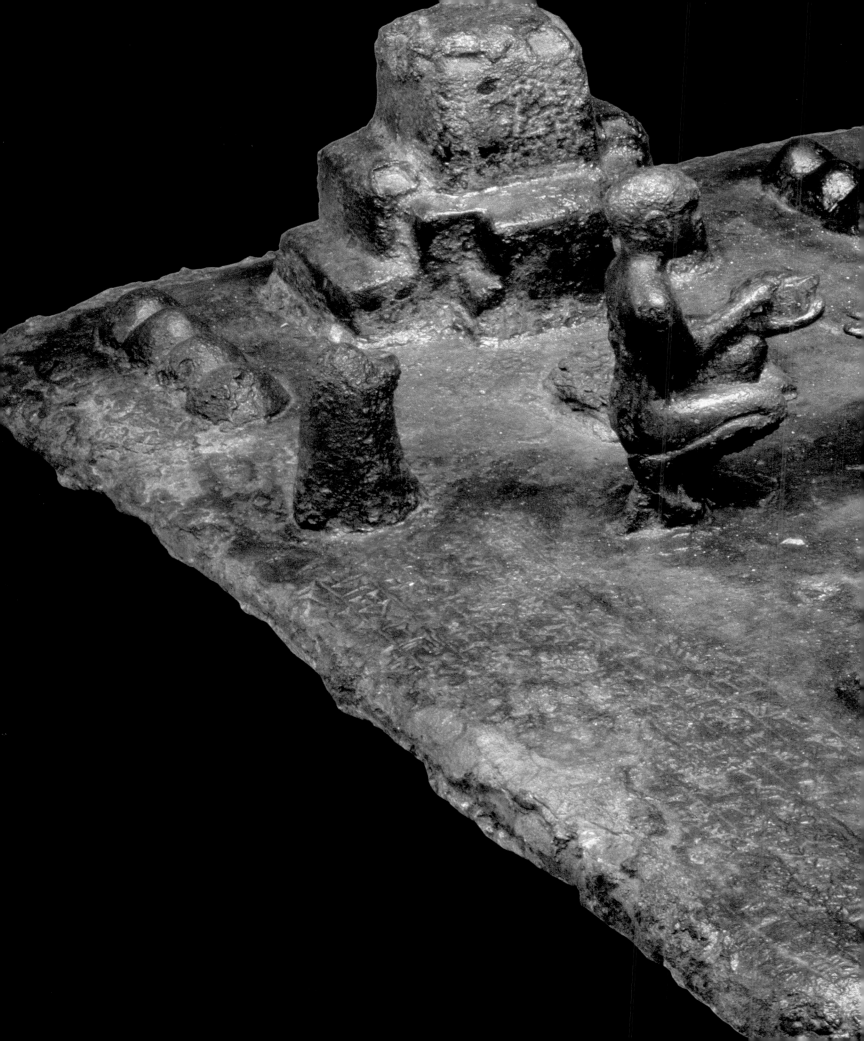

The destiny of man

The universe that emerged from the primordial separation of sky and earth, and which was governed by the community of the gods, may have seemed destined to perpetual harmony. However, the Babylonian myth of *Atra-Hasis* recounts how a spanner came to be thrown into the works:

> *"When the gods played man's role,*
> *They bore his work, carried his basket.*
> *The god's basket was very large,*
> *And the work hard: their pains were great."*

So the gods complained, and complaint soon turned to revolt. A general meeting was called, presided by Anu, so that they could decide what to do:

> *"Ea opened his mouth*
> *And spoke to the gods:*
> *There she is, Belet-ili, the divine matrix;*
> *Let the matrix bring forth, let her give form,*
> *And let man carry the basket of the gods!"*

Thus both *Atra-Hasis* and the older Sumerian myth of *Enki and Ninmah* explain man's appearance in the same way. Humanity was created in order to free the gods of their burden and act as their servants.

Most traditions also agree in their account of the way in which man was fashioned. He was formed mainly out of clay – the essential raw material of Mesopotamia – to which he would return at the end of his brief existence. In the myth of *Enki and Ninmah*, blood is mixed with lumps of clay: the mother-goddess Nammu then moulds them into a human shape. In *Atra-Hasis*, the process of creation is more complicated: the gods in one of their assemblies immolate a minor deity, Geshtu-e. His flesh and blood are then mixed with clay, and the human being thus created inherits a spark of the divine spirit.

In the period immediately following his creation, man prospered under the protection of the gods whom he served. Although mortal, human beings enjoyed a long and carefree life, safe from illness and natural calamity. This idyll, however, was soon threatened:

> *"One thousand two hundred years had not yet passed*
> *Yet the land had spread, and the people multiplied.*
> *The land roared like a herd of bulls…*
> *Enlil heard their cries*
> *And said to the great gods:*
> *The cries of humankind irritate me,*
> *I cannot sleep for their noise."*
> (Atra-Hasis.)

Enlil, the ruler of the world, seeing he could no longer control his creation, decided to destroy it. He sent down disease, drought and famine in suc-

Pages 190–191
MODEL OF THE SANCTUARY OF SIT-SHAMSI (THE RISING SUN)
Shutrukide Dynasty, Susa,
bronze,
30 x 30 cm (11 3/4 x 11 3/4 in).
Musée du Louvre, Paris.

VOTIVE STATUE OF DI-UTU
Detail. 25th-24th centuries BC,
southern Mesopotamia,
limestone,
height 27 cm (10 5/8 in).
Musée du Louvre, Paris.

NAKED PRIEST PERFORMING A LIBATION
Detail. 27th century BC, Ur,
shell plaque,
height approximately 8 cm (3 in).
British Museum, London.

cession, and only the intervention of Enki was able to save mankind from total destruction on each occasion. Enlil then decided to visit on them the supreme disaster, and called down the Flood. Before the assembly of the gods, he made Enki swear not to warn mankind. However, Enki thought up a trick that would allow him to alert his protégé, Atra-Hasis, "the most wise", without reneging on his oath. Instead of speaking directly to the man, he spoke instead to the reed wall of his house:

> "Wall, listen well:
> Reed hut, remember what I am about to tell you;
> Abandon your house, and build a boat;
> Cast off your possessions,
> And save your life!"

Atra-Hasis then spent the next seven days building a boat according to the plans laid down by Enki. When the storm came, he took his family and his animals into the boat, and while the flood ravaged the earth, and everyone else was drowned, he was able to preserve the seeds of the future of humanity. As soon as he was back on solid ground after the waters subsided, Atra-Hasis offered a meal to the gods, to prove the essential role that mankind played in the economy of the cosmos. Enlil finally accepted the renaissance of those whom he had tried to destroy, but so as to limit men's ambition, he reduced the length of their lives and introduced the hitherto unknown curses of sterility and infant mortality among them.

Thus the lot of men was determined for all time. They had to perform the tasks for which they had been formed, providing for the needs of the gods by transforming nature's resources into products fit for their consumption and by constructing buildings suitable for their worship. It was by accomplishing these tasks without fault that humanity could contribute to the harmonious working of the world.

PERFORATED WALL PLAQUE
REPRESENTING A RITUAL OFFERING

Detail. 25th-24th centuries BC,
Ur,
limestone,
height 22 cm (8 5/8 in).
British Museum, London.

The Epic of Gilgamesh

HERO MASTERING A LION
Detail, Assyrian empire,
relief from the palace of
Khorsabad
Mosul marble,
height 470 cm (15 ft).
Musée du Louvre, Paris.

HERO MASTERING A LION
Assyrian empire,
relief from the palace of Khorsabad
(formerly Dur Sharrukin),
Mosul marble,
height 545 cm (18 ft).
Musée du Louvre, Paris.

■ Mesopotamian tradition has bequeathed to us a long text of exceptional literary quality, known as the *Epic of Gilgamesh.* It is the oldest surviving epic poem. It was already famous in the ancient Near East, where it was known far beyond the limits of Mesopotamia. Its most complete version, comprising twelve tablets, was found among the ruins of the palace library at Nineveh, that had been built in the 7th century BC by the Assyrian king Ashurbanipal.

"He who has seen everything,
let me introduce him to the land…
He has contemplated mysteries
and found out secrets,
He has brought back knowledge
from before the Flood."

Thus we are introduced to Gilgamesh, who is at once a legendary figure and a historical king of Uruk. The first part of the epic relates the heroic actions of the protagonist, which embody the triumph of the civilising power of the model city of Uruk over the tumultuous forces of the untamed natural world. Gilgamesh has his double, Enkidu, who was created at the heart of the steppe by divine command. After they have fought in single combat, Enkidu enters the realm of civilisation, and the two men become inseparable. Together they undertake a journey to the distant land of the Forest of Cedars, and destroy its guardian, the giant Humbaba. Finally, back in the heart of Uruk, they defeat the heavenly bull sent by the goddess Ishtar to ravage the city.

Enkidu then dies, again by divine decision, and his death marks a turning point in the poem: however heroic a man may be, he remains a mortal whose fate lies in the hands of the gods. Gilgamesh is driven to despair and, wandering across the steppe, decides to free himself from a fate he can no longer bear. He sets off on another journey, this time to the end of the world, where he finds Uta-napishtim, the sole survivor of the Flood. He alone has the secret of "endless life". Uta-napishtim's retelling of the Flood is the dramatic high point of the work. But Gilgamesh's fate is quite different. He has to assume his mortal condition, and follow the advice given him by the inn-keeper Siduri:

"Where are you running, Gilgamesh?
The life you are looking for,
you will not find it.
When the gods created men,
They marked out death as their fate,
And life they kept in their own hands.
Gilgamesh, if your belly is full,
Give thanks day and night…
Gaze on the child who holds your hand,
And may a wife take pleasure in your arms.
These things are the business of men."

East and West: a permanent dialogue

It is difficult to know just when the cultures of Europe and the Near East first came into contact. Doubtless there was contact at the level of material culture as early as the Neolithic, as can be seen from the history of agriculture and stockbreeding. There also seems to have been contact at the level of religion during the same period: faith in the forces of fertility, as represented by the cult of the bull and the great goddess, stretched from Asia to the Balkans. During the Bronze Age, long-distance trade along the amber trade routes that led from the Baltic to the Mediterranean acted as a vector for the exchange of technical knowledge and ideas. The Homeric epics, composed in the early 1st millennium BC in the Ionian region, inherited the collective memory of a palace society, which was itself a legacy of the Bronze Age. They depict the adventures of a warrior elite, echoing the mythological narratives of the Ugarit tablets, with their sensuous evocations of heroic battles and banquets where the gods drink their fill to the sound of songs and dances accompanied by lyre, flute and cymbals. Metallurgy, the arts of fire – ceramics, faience and glass – and ivory carving (using the tusks of both the elephant and the hippopotamus) developed in parallel on either side of the Mediterranean. During the 1st millennium, Phoenician colonial expansion rivalled that of the Greek city-states, as they carved up the Mediterranean between them. But competition did not exclude exchange. One of the East's main gifts was the alphabet, adapted by the Greeks from Phoenician script, and transmitted, via the Etruscans, to Latin and all the modern languages of Europe. By extending his colonies as far as the Indus, Alexander not only brought Greece to Asia, but opened up Europe to the whole legacy of the cultures of the East.

This legacy, itself the fruit of thousands of years of cultural and commercial exchange, was conveyed above all through the works of the ancient writers. The Babylonian exile of the peoples of Syria and Israel helped introduce Mesopotamian science to the Levant. As well as astronomy and mathematics, they also brought back with them the great myths of their captors: the Biblical Flood is nothing other than a memory of a passage in the Epic of Gilgamesh. Berosus, who was born in Babylon towards the end of the 4th century BC, moved to the Greek island of Cos, where he taught the Mesopotamian tradition of astronomy. He also wrote a history of the antiquities of his homeland whose accuracy is still being borne out today by new archaeological discoveries. During the previous century, Herodotus had already composed an account of his journeys through the region,

THE CITY OF PALMYRA
1st–2nd century AD.
Palmyra, Syria.

View of the first arch of the great arcade that ran along the main street of the city.

giving his sometimes naive but always honest impressions of life in Egypt or at the court of Darius I. In the wake of the conquest of Alexander, Greek men of letters established their schools throughout the Near East, where they would prosper until the end of Antiquity. The most important of these was at Alexandria, but there were others in Antioch, Seleucia, and in the cities of the Decapolis, such as Gadara. Flavius Josephus, who was born in Jerusalem in the 1st century AD, has left us an insider's account of life in Israel during the time of Christ in his *History of the Jewish War* and *Antiquities of the Jews*. Many original texts by writers and thinkers in the Graeco-Oriental tradition have been lost, but lengthy fragments have survived in the works of Christian authors who quoted them in order to explain or refute their ideas. One such author was Clement of Alexandria (3rd century AD), the master of Origen, who was born in Alexandria and died at Tyre. In his commentaries on the Holy Scripture, he sought to reconcile Christianity with Neoplatonic thought. The writings of Eusebius (265–340), the bishop of Caesarea and valued adviser to the Emperor Constantine, are an inexhaustible source of information about the religious history of the Near East. During the Roman period, Syriac – a dialect of Aramaic – became the written language of culture alongside Greek, and Syriac-speaking theologians and philosophers played a major role in the transmission of Graeco-Oriental culture to mediaeval Europe, on the one hand, and throughout the Arab world on the other.

The case of Aristotle illustrates in exemplary fashion this mutually enriching give-and-take of cultural exchange. As Alexander the Great's master, he is rapidly translated into Latin, Syriac, Hebrew, Aramaic, and Arabic, in the wake of the emperor's conquests. Because his œuvre covered the full range of known theoretical and practical disciplines, it came to be viewed – in particular, the *Organon* – as a complete method, a theory of knowledge itself. For this reason, it was required reading for every scholar, whatever their own opinions or culture. It was debated by the Neoplatonists in Athens and added to by Syriac writers. It was the basic text of the schools of the mediaeval Latin West, just as it was received with great interest by the Abassid Arab culture and by Muslim Spain, where Averroes was cadi of the great mosque of Cordoba. Through these channels, it went on to inspire the thinkers of the European Renaissance and the philosophers of the Enlightenment.

For the West, standing on the verge of the 21st century, the cultural heritage of the ancient Near East is one of the keys to understanding the divisions that have been born out of the Judaeo-Christian Bible. But it is also the foundation of almost every discipline on which we continue to rely today in our lives, whether intellectual, technical, or artistic. As such, it is one of the most precious gifts to have been handed down to us through the ages.

TRIPYLON OF PERSEPOLIS

Achaemenid empire.

Persepolis, Iran.

King Artaxerxes I leaving his palace
accompanied by two servants.

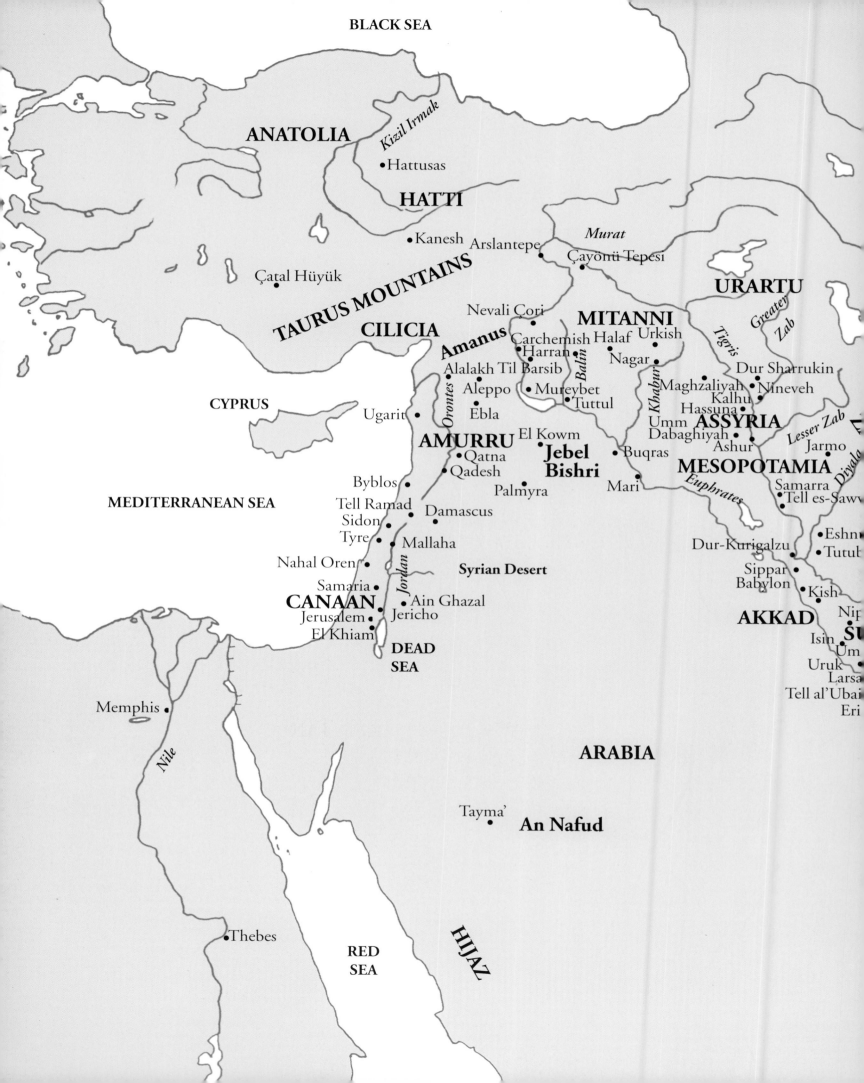

BLACK SEA

ANATOLIA

Kizil Irmak

• Hattusas

HATTI

• Kanesh Arslantepe

Murat

Çayönü Tepesi

URARTU

Greater Zab

Çatal Hüyük

TAURUS MOUNTAINS

Nevali Cori

MITANNI

Tigris

CILICIA

Amanus

Carchemish Halaf Urkish

• Dur Sharrukin

Harran

Nagar

Maghzaliyah • Nineveh

Alalakh Til Barsib

Balih

Kalhu

Aleppo • Mureybet

Hassuna

CYPRUS

Ugarit •

Orontes

Ebla

Tuttul

Umm ASSYRIA

El Kowm

Dabaghiyah

Lesser Zab

AMURRU

Jebel

Ashur Jarmo

• Qatna

Bishri

MESOPOTAMIA

Qadesh

• Buqras

Diyala

Byblos •

Palmyra

Mari

Samarra

Euphrates

MEDITERRANEAN SEA

Tell Ramad

Damascus

Tell es-Sawv

Sidon

Mallaha

Dur-Kurigalzu

Eshn

Tyre

Tutub

Jordan

Syrian Desert

Sippar

Nahal Oren

Babylon

Samaria

Ain Ghazal

AKKAD

Kish

CANAAN

Jerusalem

Jericho

Nip

Isin

Su

El Khiam

DEAD

Um

SEA

Uruk

Larsa

Tell al'Ubai

Eri

Memphis

Nile

ARABIA

Tayma'

An Nafud

Thebes

RED

HIJAZ

SEA

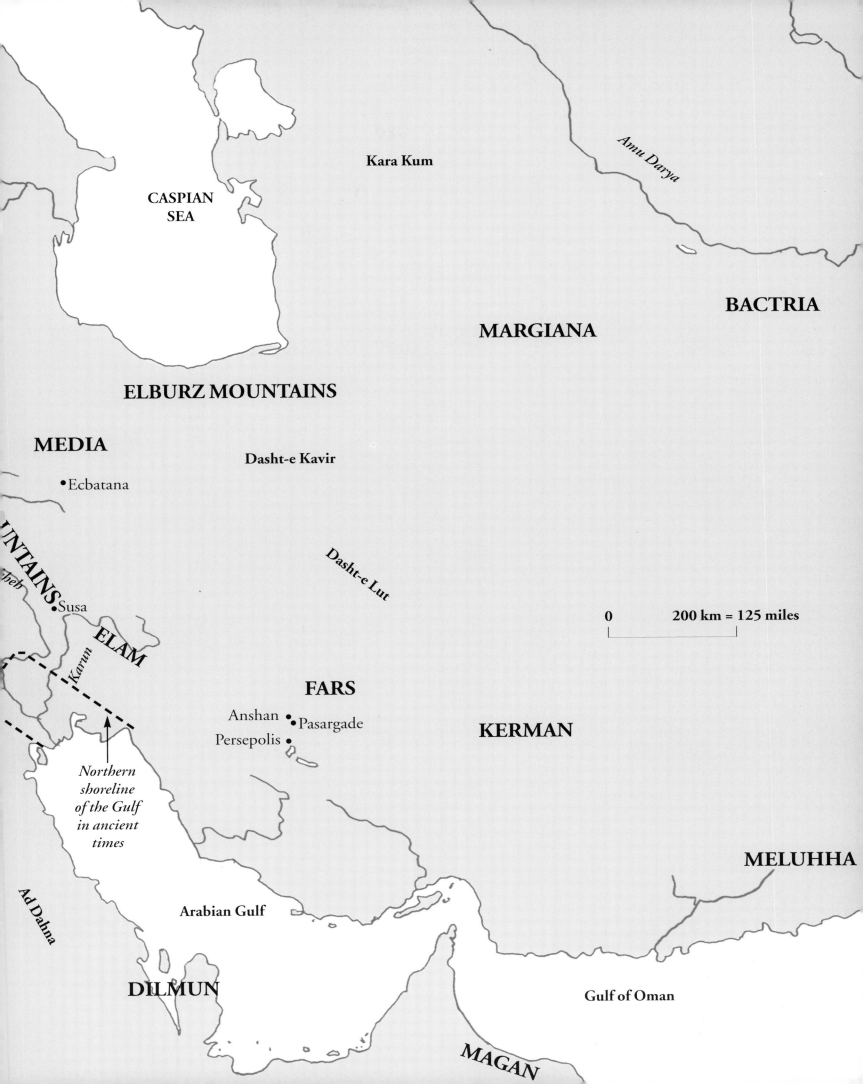

CASPIAN
SEA

Kara Kum

Amu Darya

BACTRIA

MARGIANA

ELBURZ MOUNTAINS

MEDIA

Dasht-e Kavir

•Ecbatana

Dasht-e Lut

...NTAINS
...heb
•Susa

ELAM

Karun

0   200 km = 125 miles

FARS

Anshan •
         •Pasargade
Persepolis •

KERMAN

*Northern
shoreline
of the Gulf
in ancient
times*

MELUHHA

Ad Dahna

Arabian Gulf

DILMUN

Gulf of Oman

MAGAN

LEVANT	MESOPOTAMIA	IRAN
Natufian (12,500–10,000) *		
Khiamian (10,000–9500)		
PPNA (9500–8700)	M'lefaat	
Early PPNB (8700–8200)	Nemrik	
Middle PPNB (8200–7500)		
Late PPNB (7500–7000)	Maghzaliyah	Ganj-i Dareh
		Ali Kush
		Susiana
Final PPNB (7000–6500)	Umm Dabaghiyah culture (7000–6500)	
	Hassuna culture (6500–6000) — Ubaid 0 (6500–5900)	
	Samarra culture (6200–5700) — Ubaid 1 (5900–5300)	Choga Mami
Halaf	Halaf culture (6000–5100) — Ubaid 2 (5500–5100)	
Ubaid	Northern Ubaid — Ubaid 3 (5300–4700)	
	Ubaid 4 (4700–4200)	
	Ubaid 5 (4200–3700)	Susa I (4000–3500)
	Early Uruk (3700–3400)	
	Middle Uruk (3400–3100)	Susa II (3500–3100)
	Late Uruk (3100–2900)	Susa III (3100–2700)
	ARCHAIC SUMERIAN DYNASTIES (2900–2330)	
	Mebaragesi, king of Kish (c. 2700)	Susa IV (2700–2200)
	Gilgamesh, king of Uruk	
	Meskalamdug, king of Ur (c. 2600)	
	Mesanepada, king of Ur	
EBLA	MARI — Mesilim, king of Kish (c. 2550)	
	Ishgi-Mari — Ur-Nanshe, king of Lagash (c. 2500)	
Igrish-Halam	Iblul-Il — Eannatum, king of Lagash (c. 2450)	
Irkab-Damu	Enna-Dagan — Entemena, king of Lagash (c. 2400)	AWAN DYNASTY (c. 2400)
Ish'ar-Damu	Uruinimgina, king of Lagash (c. 2350)	
	Lugalzagesi, king of Umma	
	AKKADIAN DYNASTY	
	Sargon (2334–2279)	
	Rimush (2278–2270)	
	Manishtushu (2269–2255)	
	Naram-Sin (2254–2218)	
	Shar-kali-sharri (2217–2193)	
	SECOND DYNASTY OF LAGASH	
	Gudea (2125–2110)	
	THIRD DYNASTY OF UR	
	MARI — Ur-Nammu (2112–2095)	Puzur-Inshushinak, king of Awan and of Susa (c. 2100)
Ibdati, king of Byblos (c. 2050)	Shakkanakku Dynasty — Shulgi (2094–2047)	SHIMASHKI DYNASTY
	(c. 2100) — Amar-Sin (2046–2038)	Kindattu (c. 2005)
	Shu-Sin (2037–2029)	
	Ibbi-Sin (2028–2004)	
	DYNASTIES OF ISIN AND LARSA	SUKKALMAH DYNASTY
	Ishbi-Erra, king of Isin (2017–1985)	Ebarat (c. 1970)
	Lipit-Ishtar, king of Isin (1934–1924)	Attahushu (c. 1927)
	Gungunum, king of Larsa (1932–1906)	
	Rim-Sin, king of Larsa (1822–1763)	
	MARI — ASSYRIA	
	Iakhdun-Lim (1815–1799) — Puzur-Ashur	
	Zimri-Lim (1775–1762) — Erishum I (c. 1940)	
	Shamsi-Adad (1810–1776)	
Yarim-Lim I, king of Aleppo (1780–1765)		
Amut-pi-El, king of Qatna	FIRST DYNASTY OF BABYLON	
Yantinhammu, king of Byblos	Sumu-abum (1894–1881)	
	Hammurabi (1792–1750)	
HITTITE OLD KINGDOM	Samsu-iluna (1749–1712)	
Hattusilis I (1650–1620)	Samsu-ditana (1625–1595)	
Mursilis I (1620–1590)		
	KASSITE DYNASTY OF BABYLON	
Telepinu (1525–1500)	Agum kakrime (c. 1595)	
	Burnaburiash I (c. 1500)	
Idrimi, king of Alalakh (c. 1500)		
MITANNI		IGI-HALKIDE DYNASTY
Parrattarna I (c. 1500)		Igi-Halki (1400–1380)
Saustatar (c. 1450)	Kara-indash (c. 1415)	Untash-Napirisha (1340–1300)
Tushratta (c. 1370)	Kurigalzu I (c. 1380)	
	Burnaburiash II (1359–1333)	
	Kashtiliashu IV (1232–1225)	
	Meli-Shipak II (1185–1171)	
NEO-HITTITE EMPIRE	ASSYRIA	
Shuppiluliuma I (1370–1335)	Ashuruballit I (1365–1330)	
Muwatallis II (1305–1282)	Adadnirari I (1307–1275)	
Hattusilis III (1275–1250)	Shalmaneser I (1274–1245)	
Tudhaliya IV (1250–1220)	Tukulti-Ninurta I (1244–1208)	
Ammurapi, last king of Ugarit (c. 1200)	Tiglath-pileser I (1115–1077)	

LEVANT	MESOPOTAMIA	IRAN
		SHUTRUKIDE DYNASTY Shutruk-Nahhunte (1190–1155) Kudur-Nahhunte (1155–1150) Shilhak-Inshushinak (1150–1120)
	SECOND DYNASTY OF ISIN Nebuchadnezzar I (1124–1103)	
Ahiram, king of Byblos (c. 1000) David, king of Israel (1010–970) Solomon, king of Israel (970–931) Hiram I, king of Tyre (969–935)	ASSYRIAN EMPIRE Ashurdan II (934–912) Adadnirari II (911–891) Tukulti-Ninurta II (890–884) Ashurnasirpal II (883–859) Shalmaneser III (858–824)	
Hadad-Ezer, king of Damascus (c. 850) Jehu, king of Israel (841–814)	Shamsi-Adad V (823–811) Adadnirari III (810–783) Tiglath-pileser III (744–727) Shalmaneser V (726–722)	Cyaxares, king of the Medes (653–585)
Sarduri II, king of Urartu (c. 740) Rusa I, king of Urartru (719–713) Mita, king of Phrygia Hezekiah, king of Judah (719–699)	Sargon II (721–705) Sennacherib (704–681) Esarhaddon (680–669) Ashurbanipal (668–629)	Astyages, king of the Medes (585–550)
	CHALDEAN DYNASTY OF BABYLON Nabopolassar (625–605) Nebuchadnezzar II (604–562) Nabonidos (556–539)	ACHAEMENID DYNASTY Cyrus II (559–530) Cambyses II (530–522) Darius I (522–486) Xerxes I (486–465) Artaxerxes I (465–424) Artaxerxes II (404–359) Darius III (336–330)
* All dates are BC		Alexander of Macedon

FROM PICTOGRAPHS TO CUNEIFORM

	Pictographic sign c. 3100 BC	Cuneiform sign c. 2400 BC	Cuneiform sign c. 700 BC	Sumerian transliteration	Meaning
Star				an, dingir	sky, god
Sun				Ud, U_4	sun, day
Bull's head				gu_4	bull, ox
Cow's head				ab_2	cow
Man's body				lu_2	man
Human head and bowl				ku_2	to eat
Ear of wheat				she	grain
Woman				munus	woman

BIBLIOGRAPHY

Black, J., and Green, A., *Gods, Demons and Symbols of Ancient Mesopotamia. An Illustrated Dictionary,* London, 1992.

Bottéro, J., Cassin, E., and Vercoutter, E., *The Near East: the Early Civilisations,* London, 1967.

Cambridge History of the Ancient World, ed. I.E.S. Edwards, C.J. Gadd, N.G.L. Hammond, E. Sollberger, 3rd edition, Cambridge, 1970.

Collon, D., *Ancient Near Eastern Art,* London, 1995.

Dalley, S. (tr.), *Myths from Mesopotamia,* Oxford, 1989.

Frankfort, H., *The Art and Architecture of the Ancient Orient,* Pelican History of Art, Harmondsworth, 1954 (revd. edition, 1970).

Gurney, O.R., *The Hittites,* Harmondsworth, 1952 (revd. edition, 1981, 1990).

Sandars, N.K. (tr.), *The Epic of Gilgamesh,* Harmondsworth, 1960 (revd. edition, 1964, 1972).

Lloyd, S., *Ancient Turkey: A Traveller's History of Anatolia,* London, 1989 (revd. edition, 1992).

Oates, D. and J., *The Rise of Civilization,* Oxford, 1976.

Oates, J., *Babylon,* London, 1979 (revd. edition, 1986).

Postgate, J.N., *Early Mesopotamia: Society and Economy at the Dawn of History,* London, 1992.

Roux, G., *Ancient Iraq,* Harmondsworth, 1966 (revd. edition, 1986).

Russell, J.M., *Sennacherib's Palace without Rival at Nineveh,* Chicago, 1991.

AKG, Berlin: pp. 106-107, 138-139, 139 (right). Bildarchiv Preussischer Kulturbesitz, Berlin: pp. 18-19, 34 (bottom), 35, 91, 112-113, 136 (bottom left), 136 (bottom right), 156-157. British Museum, London: pp. 2, 12, 13, 24, 39, 60-61 (top and bottom), 62-63, 111, 122, 122-123, 124-125, 126, 128 (bottom), 130-131 (top), 132, 133, 152-153, 154 (top and bottom), 160-161, 189, 194-195. CNRS, Mureybet mission, Jales: p. 20. CNRS, Mureybet mission, Jales, A. Bedos: pp. 21 and 22. Dagli Orti, Paris: pp. 25, 28-29, 30, 32, 33, 48, 49, 59 (right), 76, 77, 142, 181, 184-185. Explorer, Paris, Fiore: pp. 86-87, 200-201. Explorer, Paris, C. Lenars: p. 127. Explorer, Paris, G. Thouvenin: pp. 136 (top) and 137. Hirmer Verlag, Munich: p. 34 (top). Musée du Louvre, Department of Near Eastern Antiquities, Paris: pp. 70, 71, 92-93, 121 (left and right), 128 (left), 129 (top and bottom), 174, 175, 196, 197. Musée du Louvre, Ali Meyer: cover, pp. 5, 6, 14-15, 16, 26, 27 (top), 36, 37, 38 (top and bottom), 40, 41, 42-43, 44, 45, 46 (left and right), 47, 52-53, 54, 56, 58, 59 (left), 64, 65, 66, 67, 68, 69, 72, 73, 74-75, 78, 79, 80, 81, 82 (left and right), 83, 84-85, 85 (right), 90, 94, 95, 96, 97, 98-99, 100, 101, 102 (left), 102-103, 104, 109, 110, 114, 116, 118, 119, 120, 128 (top right), 130 (bottom), 131 (top and bottom), 134, 135, 140, 141, 144-145 (top and bottom), 146, 147, 148, 149, 150 (top and bottom), 151 (left and right), 155, 158, 159, 162, 163, 164, 165, 166, 168 (left), 168-169, 170-171, 172, 173, 176-177, 178-179 (top), 178-179 (bottom), 180, 182, 183, 186 (left), 186-187, 188 (top and right), 192, 193. Musée du Louvre, Frank Lachenet: pp. 8-9, 10-11, 23, 55, 108, 115, 117, 199. Musée du Louvre, John Tsantes: p. 27 (bottom). Oriental Institute Museum, Chicago, Victor J. Boswell: p. 57. Rapho, Paris, Gerster: pp. 88-89. Robert Harding, London: p. 50 (top and bottom). RMN, Paris: pp. 190-191.

In the same series:

ANCIENT
CIVILIZATIONS

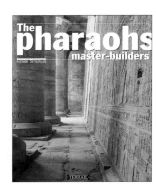

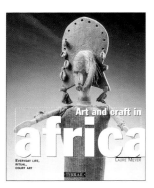

PRIMITIVE ARTS

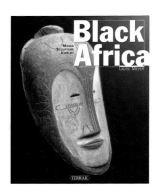

ARCHITECTURE
- Classical Modern Architecture
- Jean Nouvel
- Architecture of today
- Architecture for the future

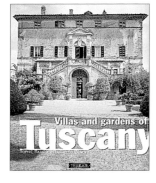

CITIES OF ART
- Rome – Palaces and Gardens
- Villas and Gardens of Tuscany
- The Glory of Venice
- Florence and the Renaissance

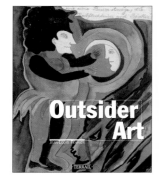

PAINTING SCULPTURE
- Outsider Art
- Duchamp & Co.
- Picasso
- Paris-Montparnasse
- Paris-Montmartre
- Kandinsky
- Modigliani
- The Fauves
- Gauguin and the Nabis
- Rodin
- Mucha
- Caspar David Friedrich
- Masters of English Landscape
- Michelangelo
- Leonardo
- Early Flemish Painting